LoGO

LoGO

Mike Lowe

FEEDAREAD

Published in 2016 by FeedARead.com Publishing

Copyright   Mike Lowe

The author has asserted his moral right under the
Copyright, Designs and Patents Act, 1988, to be identified
as the author of this work.

A CIP catalogue record for this title is available from
the British Library

for George

Also by Mike Lowe

Milvar's Path
Going Dutch
Hermit
Banger

1

When Mervyn saw the dilapidated state of the building he thought the taxi must have dropped him off at the wrong place. The building looked almost derelict, paint was peeling from the window frames, the brickwork was patchy and damp-stained, and the roof looked in need of some new slates. The grass verges were overgrown and someone had dumped an old mattress in the ditch near the entrance. But a crooked sign read, "Councillor William Hardcastle House – A Division of Hindthorpe Borough Council". That was the address on his letter of appointment so it must be right. He consulted the letter again. 'Report to Cyril Openthwaite at Councillor William Hardcastle House at 9 am on Monday 5th January.'

He really wasn't sure about this job. He'd applied for it because it was one of very few advertised that he thought he might possibly have a chance of getting. He'd tried so many different things in his short life and none of them had really suited him. 'What do you want to do when you grow up, or leave school?' people always asked, and he had never been able to answer. He still couldn't. He simply didn't know what he wanted to do. But he had to do something. He'd never been to this rather dismal town before and he had not been impressed by what he had seen of it from the windows of the train and later, the taxi. Rows and rows of terraced red brick houses and buildings that had once been factories – nothing much was made here any more – so what went on in those satanic mills now?

Still, he was here now, they'd offered him the job and he'd been glad to accept. Perhaps it would work out.

'Here goes,' he said to himself, and walked up the short drive to the front door.

The door opened on to a dark lobby with decorative Victorian tiles on the floor and walls. A large notice board, headed with the Borough Council logo, announced a number of events, some of which had passed long before. A narrow staircase seemed the only option since the only doors in the lobby were to men's and women's toilets. Mervyn climbed the bare wooden stairs with some trepidation.

At the top of the stairs, a landing with four unmarked doors, all of which were closed, did nothing to reassure him. However, just then, one of the doors opened and an untidy but genial looking man in jeans and a black sweatshirt bearing the council logo emerged

'Oh, hello. Can I help?'

'Hello, yes, I hope so; I am looking for Mr Cyril Openthwaite. I'm the new Community Liaison Officer,' said Mervyn, offering his hand, 'Mervyn Davis'.

'He's not in yet, I'm George, caretaker and general dogsbody. Don't worry, I'll show you your desk and get you a cuppa – what do you fancy, tea or coffee?' He led the way to the end of the landing where a door bearing a post-it label stuck to the top panel read, 'Liaison Office – Come in'

George pushed open the door and ushered Mervyn inside. The office didn't inspire confidence. The walls were painted an unpleasant shade of yellow that had faded to brown in places and a patched orange carpet covered most of the floor. Two old wooden desks, set at right angles to each other, dominated the room. There were two notice boards and a cursory glance was enough for Mervyn to see that many of the notices were out of date. The larger of the two desks was placed so that the person sitting at it could look out of the window at a landscape of high-rise blocks of flats, a distant glimpse of trees and the faintest sparkle of water. Immediately below the window was a children's playground with swings and a seesaw. Two small children were playing and two young women sat watching them.

'That's your desk, Mr, er . . .'

'Mervyn, please. Thanks.' Mervyn put his brand new briefcase on the desk and looked for somewhere to hang his coat.

'You can hang your coat behind the door if you like, or there is a cupboard if you'd rather.'

'No, the door is fine,' said Mervyn, hanging his coat on the solitary hook.

'I'll get that coffee then, you did say coffee? How do you like it? I don't think we've any milk.'

'Black is fine, thank you.'

'We don't say 'black', we say 'without milk,'' said George hesitantly.

'Oh? Oh, I see, right oh. Without milk then, thanks.'

'Good, because we don't usually have any milk, but you can always go to the shop for some if you do want it.'

'Where is the shop? Just in case I need something.'

'Just across the road, you'll see it – Singh's Emporium. They sell everything and stay open late as well.'

George went out, leaving Mervyn to take stock of his new surroundings. The office could do with smartening up but that could wait until he had settled in. The desk was somewhat battered but it had several drawers which could be useful, and there was even a telephone and a small dog-eared book, bearing the hand-written legend 'Council Numbers'.

The chair was of the swivelling variety and had several adjustments allowing the user to alter the height and rake of the seat. Mervyn took a few minutes of fiddling to get the chair to suit him and by that time George had reappeared with two mugs of coffee.

'Cracker?' asked George.

'I beg your pardon?'

'Cracker? Do you like cracker biscuits?'

'Yes, I quite like them.'

'I've usually got a supply – you've only to ask,' said George, as he sat at the other desk and produced a packet of cracker biscuits from a drawer. 'Want one?'

'Thank you, that's kind.'

'That's OK. Next time you go to Singh's you can get a packet and we can share.' He munched on dry crackers for several minutes in comparative silence. 'Do you normally have butter on yours?'

'What? Oh, well, yes I do usually, and a bit of cheese.'

'I like them just as they are. You'll get used to them like that.'

Mervyn realised that he was expected to eat his cracker biscuit without butter and cheese and supposed he could get used to them like that.

'When did you say Mr Openthwaite was expected?'

'I didn't. He might not come in today as it's a Monday.'

'Oh, but I was supposed to report to him, you see.'

'That's OK, you've reported to me. I'll show you the ropes.'

'Doesn't he come in on Mondays then?'

'Not if it's the first week in the month. He goes up north every month, to see his mother, and if it's the first weekend in the month he doesn't come in on the Monday. It is the first weekend in the month isn't it?'

'Yes, it is, and the first weekend in the year.'

'Oh yes, well there you are then. He won't be in. Don't worry. You'll see him soon enough, I dare say.'

'I don't know what I'm supposed to do,' said Mervyn, weakly.

'Oh, don't worry; you'll soon get the hang of it. I'll fill you in as we go along.'

The phone rang.

'I'll get it,' said George, reaching across for the phone on Mervyn's desk.

'Hello, yes, this is the Liaison Office, yes, yes. Oh, right, I understand. Leave it with me then. Bye.'

He sat back at his desk and continued to drink his coffee and munch on another biscuit.

'What was that about?' asked Mervyn.

'What, the phone? Urgent repairs needed in one of the towers. Water coming through the ceiling. Happens all the time.'

'So, what are you going to do about it?'

'I'll get the maintenance crew out – when I've had my coffee.'

Several minutes went by before George stood up and took the empty coffee mugs away. He could be heard somewhere near, clattering – presumably washing the mugs. When he came back, he smiled brightly. 'We can start the day now we've had our coffee. Where was I?'

'The phone call?'

'Oh, yes. Pass me the phone.'

He dialled a number, 'Hardeep? Yes, George. Water coming through the ceiling in Harding Tower. Number three hundred and two. Can you see to it? Yes, well, I meant after you've had your coffee. Right oh, then, thanks. Bye.'

'That was Hardeep, he runs the maintenance crew. Nice chap. Do anything for you. Incidentally, where are you living? Have you got somewhere local?'

'As a matter of fact I'm going to be moving in to a flat in Wilson Tower – on the fifteenth floor, just until I find something more permanent. The housing department sorted it for me.'

'They're OK, the flats, when you get used to being up in the sky. Don't try to move any big furniture in though, there's only the passenger lift apart from the stairs, and if you're up fifteen floors you won't want to hump much up there.'

'No, I suppose not. I think I shall have everything I need for a short stay.'

'Good view though, from up there.'

'Yes, I guess I'll be able to see the whole town from up there.'

'Best way to see it,' said George, enigmatically.

'So, what's the drill then, George?'

'Drill? The job, you mean?'

'Yes, what does the department actually do? It was very vague in the advert for the job and I didn't learn a lot from the interview.'

'Didn't you ask? It's a bit risky taking on a job if you don't know what you're supposed to do, isn't it?'

'I did ask, of course, but they seemed to think that with my experience I wouldn't have any trouble and left it at that.'

'Mm. Who was on the panel?'

'Councillor Matthews was the chairman and then there was the head of the Community Amenities Department and a couple of women who didn't introduce themselves.'

'Typical,' said George.

'What do you mean?'

'Well, they usually have a couple of people from the residents' committees on interview panels, just to make it democratic.'

'I see,' said Mervyn, beginning to wonder what sort of outfit he had got himself into. 'So, what does the department do, George?'

'We sort out council house residents' complaints and stuff like that most of the time. They come to us if they have a problem with anything – like the one we had this morning – water leaks. They're the most common in the towers. They weren't built right in the first place. The central heating – good idea – everybody having heating provided of course, but it doesn't work all that well. Hardeep – the maintenance man – I told you about him? Well, he is based in the West Tower so as to be on the spot when the trouble occurs. It is a pretty much full time job. Then there's the committees, you'll be on most of those. Then there's looking after the community centres and the swimming pool, when it's working, and the tennis courts – taking bookings and that. Then in the summer, there's the shows and concerts, we do all that.'

'Gosh, I had no idea you did all that. How many people are on the staff?'

George laughed, so much that he sprayed the room with cracker biscuit crumbs and nearly choked. 'The staff,' he said, gasping for breath, is you! I help out of course, and there's His Nibs, but he's so rarely here, you can't really count him. There are lots of different departments you can call on for help of course – once you get to know them.'

'His Nibs, I suppose you mean Cyril Openthwaite?'

'Yes, him. He's OK. Nice enough guy, but not a lot of help in a crisis, if you know what I mean.'

'Well, no, I don't really.'

'You'll see,' said George, smiling as he nibbled on yet another cracker biscuit.

'And we just sit here and wait for the calls to come in do we?'

'Well, there's no point in going looking for work is there?'

Mervyn went over George's last comment in his mind and just as he was thinking he would have to say something to break the uncomfortable silence, the telephone rang again. He picked it up.

'Hello, Liaison Department. Can I help you?'

'Who is that? Is George there?' said the voice on the phone.

'This is Mervyn Davis, the new Liaison Officer. Who am I speaking to?'

10

'Matthews. Well done lad, you've got on the job already. That is splendid. Come and see me at the Town Hall for a chat. How about tomorrow?'

'Yes, tomorrow will be fine, what time? Ten o'clock, yes of course, thank you, Mr Matthews, goodbye.' He put down the handset.

'You should call him Councillor,' said George.

'What?'

'Was that Councillor Matthews?'

'Somebody called Matthews – he wants to see me.'

'Yes, Councillor Matthews. You have to call them all Councillor. You weren't to know of course, but you'd better remember in future.'

'I will. Who is he anyway?'

'He's the one who interviewed you isn't he, that's what you said.'

'Oh, yes, of course. I shall know him when I see him. Where do I go in the Town Hall? He wants to see me tomorrow morning.'

'Do you know where the Town Hall is?'

'Yes, that's where I went for my interview.'

'Just ask Harry on the door, he'll show you where to go.'

Mervyn was thinking about his impending chat with the councillor when the door burst open and a flustered young woman came into the office.

'George? Oh? Sorry, are you busy?'

'This is our new Liaison Officer, Mervyn – '

'Davis, Mervyn Davis,' offered Mervyn.

'Oh, Hi, I'm Vanessa, I work in the swimming pool. Excuse me, this is rather urgent. George, can you get on to Hardeep for me? All the water has drained out of the pool and we have a gala at the weekend and people want to practice.'

'Well, if all the water has gone, it will take a week to fill it, so they won't be able to practice. Can't they go somewhere else?'

'I know, but I've got to do something. Please George, Hardeep will do it for you,' she pleaded, looking at George with big puppy eyes.

'Of course I'll ask him. I doubt he'll be able to do much though. Do you want a cuppa while you're here?'

'No, ring him now, please, George.'

'OK, ok, if you insist. Pass me the phone, Merv.'

'I would prefer to be called Mervyn if you don't mind, George.'

'OK.' He picked up the phone and dialled a short number. 'Hardeep? Hi, it's George again. Have you sorted that leak? Yes, well you were having coffee last time I spoke to you. Well, do it as quick as you can, please. And there's another crisis now. The pool has sprung a leak. Can you see to that as well? It is pretty urgent.

Thanks a lot, Hardeep.' He turned to Vanessa, 'He's a good man. He'll be right there. Meet him out front in half an hour. OK?'

'Oh, thanks, George. I knew you'd be able to persuade him. See you then. I'll catch you another time Mervyn, Bye!' and she was gone, clattering down the uncarpeted stairs in her high heels.

'It's all go, isn't it,' said Mervyn, somewhat ill advisedly.

'What do you mean?' asked George, not catching Mervyn's inflection.

2

The imposing red-brick Town Hall, headquarters of the Borough Council, was in the centre of the old part of the town where parking was virtually impossible. However there was a space right in front of the building, and Mervyn gratefully slid his ten year old SAAB into it. He looked round for a parking meter and finding none, locked the car and began to walk away.

'Oi! You can't leave it there!' came a shout behind Mervyn's left ear. He turned to see a large uniformed woman hurrying towards him, wielding a notebook and pen.

'I'm sorry, were you talking to me?' he asked, innocently.

'Yes, I was. You can't leave your car there. Move it.'

'I have business at the Town Hall . . .'

'I don't care if you have business with the Queen herself, sunshine, you ain't leavin' it there.'

'But where should I park then? That looked to me the sort of place one would park if one had business in the Town Hall.'

'Perhaps it would if you was the ruddy Mayor. That's 'is spot.'

'There is nothing to indicate that it is reserved for anyone.'

'You're not from round 'ere are you?'

'I work here, but no, I am not a native.'

'What are you implying – that I am a savage or somethin'?'

'No, what I mean is I was not born here. But what that has to do with anything, I fail to understand, and if you keep me much longer I shall be late for my appointment with Councillor Matthews. Now, please, I must get on.'

'Oh, name dropping now are we. Well that doesn't wash with me. I shall have to issue you with a ticket.' With that she scribbled something on a yellow ticket, placed it inside a plastic envelope and stuck it firmly on the SAAB's windscreen.

'Thank you. I wish you good day,' said Mervyn as calmly as possible, and walked off towards the Town Hall.

'You can pay the fine while you're in there!' shouted the traffic warden. But Mervyn ignored her and continued up the steps to the big studded doors.

'Good Morning, Sir. They'll tow your car away, you know, if you don't move it,' said the doorman, emerging from his cubby-hole by the door.

15

'What? But I have a ticket already . . .'

'Yes, but you've parked in the Mayor's space, and that is not allowed.'

'Look, I have an appointment with Councillor Matthews and if I waste any more time I shall be late. Please tell me where I can find him.'

'First floor, room number eleven. Mr Davis, is it?'

'Yes, that's right,' said Mervyn, surprised.

'You're expected, go on up.' The doorman smiled and retreated into his cubby-hole.

Councillor Matthews was waiting for Mervyn at the door of Room eleven. He smiled and extended his hand. 'Good to see you Davis, come on in. Take a seat.'

'Thank you, Councillor, good morning.'

'Got off to a bad start there, parking in the Mayor's spot. I saw you from the window. I'm afraid it'll cost you thirty quid for the fine and if you aren't out of here inside an hour they'll tow your car away and you'll have to pay them to get it back.' The councillor was smiling. He evidently did not regard the parking offence seriously.

'But can't I get the fine rescinded as I was here to see you on official business?'

'Not really, but as it's your first week, I suppose I could see what can be done. Now, coffee?'

'Oh, yes, thank you.'

The councillor picked up one of several telephones and asked for two coffees to be sent up. 'Room service,' he chuckled. 'I'll watch the time, so you can be out in time to collect your car before the tow truck comes. Now, how are you finding things?'

'I've hardly had time to get my bearings, let alone get to grips with the job, to be honest. Mr Openthwaite isn't in this week so I haven't had an induction or anything.'

'No, well, perhaps I can help you there. I could show you round if you like, introduce you to some of the staff and tell you a little about what we do in the department.'

'That would be wonderful. I was thinking I might have to find out what's what from George.'

'Oh, well you could do worse than hear it from George, he's been around longer than any one else on the council. Knows everybody and is owed a favour by almost everybody!' The councillor laughed heartily.

Coffee arrived on a silver tray, borne by a very attractive young lady in a dark green suit that looked like an air hostess's uniform.

'There you are, Councillor. Shall I pour for you?' she asked.

'That's OK, Sandra, thank you. Did you bring any biscuits?'

'Oh, no, sorry. I'll get some.' She scuttled away and the councillor turned to Mervyn and smiled. 'They pick 'em for their looks, I swear.'

They sat drinking their coffee for several minutes and waited in vain for the biscuits, before the councillor spoke.

'So, tell me about yourself. I know you told us at the interview but, to be honest, we saw so many people that day I've forgotten most of it. Congratulations, by the way, you were the best candidate.

Mervyn gave the councillor a potted history of his previous employments, including his time in the army and the year he spent selling expensive leather luggage in Saudi Arabia. The councillor raised his eyebrows at that one. He described his varied interests and said how much he was looking forward to working for the borough council.

'What is it that attracted you to this job, Davis?' asked the councillor, when Mervyn's account dried up.

'I like people and I like variety. The job description sounded ideal for me. It would seem that no two days are the same, and I like a challenge.'

'Well, that's good because the job is a challenge. You see we've only just created this job; it is a bit of an experiment to be truthful. The department covers such a lot of different services that we thought we needed someone to hang it all together as it were, that's why we called it liaison, you see. I just hope you'll be able to develop it yourself. I am not your boss of course, but I would appreciate it if you keep me informed. It's my baby in a way.'

'Yes, of course. I'll be happy to keep you informed of my progress.'

'Let's meet again tomorrow and I'll show you round. Ten o'clock then, but not here. Let's say the Transport Yard. You'll be wanting to pick up your car anyway, won't you?'

'Oh, do I get a car?'

'Of course, dear boy. We can't have a council officer driving round in an old banger like yours can we!' He laughed, slapping Mervyn on the back. 'Off you go, take care now.'

'Thank you, Councillor. I'll see you tomorrow.'

Mervyn left the Town Hall with a smile on his face. They were giving him a car! He wondered what it would be. He loved his old SAAB but it had to be said it was getting a bit tired having done more than a quarter of a million miles. He could never part with it of course, but it would be nice to have a new car. He had never had a brand new car and he could hardly contain his excitement at the prospect.

His SAAB was still in the prohibited parking bay when he reached it, and the ticket was still on the windscreen. He snatched the offending article and threw it into the car and, still smiling, drove off, rather too fast.

Back at his office, he asked George where the Transport Department was and George kindly offered to show him in the morning.

'What are you getting?' George wanted to know.

'I don't know, what do they usually provide?'

'I've no idea. I don't qualify myself and I don't know anyone in the department who has a company car. You are obviously one of the chosen people. Do you fancy a cuppa?'

'Good idea, George. I bought some cracker biscuits on the way.'

'Oh, great, I've run out.'

George made coffee and they munched on the newly provided cracker biscuits, thinking about company cars.

3

George was as good as his word and was ready at nine o'clock to show Mervyn where the transport department was.

The very large yard, surrounded by old red brick buildings must once have been a railway goods yard; traces of railway tracks could still be seen in the tarmac and some of the buildings had large arched doorways, big enough for goods wagons to enter. Newer buildings provided cover for lorries and vans, a few minibuses and several small saloon cars.

'This is where they service all the council vehicles, they'll do your private ones as well once you get to know the guys. I always get mine done here. It's a lot cheaper than the commercial garages,' said George, as he waved to a man in dirty blue overalls, coming out of the largest building which seemed to be full of snowploughs.

'Do you get a lot of snow here, George? I've never seen so many snowploughs,' said Mervyn.

'Not all that much. They hire them out to other councils, very lucrative it is too. They

21

over-ordered a few years ago and Paul, the man in charge, was given the push over it. But then when someone had the bright idea of hiring them out Paul was taken back on as the hero of the day. He's still here.'

'Where do you think I should wait for Councillor Matthews? He said meet him here but it is a huge place. I could miss him.'

'No, you won't miss him. We'll just wait by the cash office – that's where you go for your expenses by the way.'

'Expenses? What sort of expenses?'

'Oh, you'll get to know all about expenses,' laughed George, with a twinkle in his eye. 'Just don't overdo it, that's all. I'll explain it all to you when we get back to the office. Oh, look, here's the councillor's car now.' He pointed to a large dark blue Jaguar, coming into the yard.

'Do you think that's a company car, George?' asked Mervyn.

'No, funnily enough, councillors don't get all that many perks. That'll be his car. He has his own company you know. They make industrial clothing and safety equipment.'

'And provide the council, no doubt,' surmised Mervyn.

'You got it. He's OK though, best of the bunch.'

The councillor spotted Mervyn and George and drove over towards them, stopped just a few yards away and got out of the car.

'Davis! And George, jolly good. I guess you'll have shown Mr Davis the way. Thank you, George. You can get off now if you like. We'll be OK now.' The councillor politely dismissed George, who began to move away.

'Oh, George!' called Mervyn. Do you want to take my car back to the office?' He threw the keys to George's outstretched hand.

'Thanks. I'll see you later then. Bye. Bye, Councillor.'

'Good man, George, said the councillor, as he steered Mervyn towards the cash office. 'This is where they do all the insurance for the council vehicles. You'll need to do some paperwork and then we can go and pick up your new car.'

Mervyn was introduced to the people in the cash office and handed a wadge of forms to complete. When he had completed them the clerk handed him an envelope and asked him to keep a record of the mileage each week and to bring in his travelling expenses claim form. 'You know where to go, don't you?'

'It's all right Maisie, I'll show him,' assured the councillor. 'Come on, Davis, we'll go in the Jag.'

Mervyn had been expecting to pick up his car at the depot so he was very surprised when they drove to a dealership on the outskirts of the town. The car park was full of gleaming new cars and Mervyn wondered which of them might be his.

'Here we are, just hand over your paperwork to the man at the desk and he'll sort you out,' said the councillor, smiling benignly. 'I'll wait for you here, and then we'll go in convoy back to your office before I show you some more of the department.'

Mervyn could hardly believe his good fortune when he was shown his new car – a shiny blue Volkswagen Golf. It took no more than a few minutes for the car to be handed over to him. He joined the councillor in front of the building, looking like the cat that had just swallowed the canary.

'All done?' asked the councillor, looking almost as pleased.

'Yes, what do you think?' Mervyn asked, pointing at the new car. 'It's a beauty.'

'Very nice indeed. I wish you happy motoring. Now, what I suggest is we take your car back to the office and I'll show you round the department's main sites and introduce you to your colleagues.'

'Sounds good, thank you very much.'

'That's OK, as I said, this post of yours is really my baby, so I want it to work. I'll help you all I can.'

The first stop after they had driven back to Hardcastle house to leave the new car, was the swimming pool. Mervyn had already met Vanessa and she greeted him with a wave as they went through the turnstile at the entrance.

'You know Miss Turton, do you?' asked the councillor, surprised.

'Yes, she called in to see George, yesterday.'

'Perhaps she'll show us round then – Miss Turton? Have got a minute?' he called.

Vanessa said she could spare them a few minutes now that the pool was filling up. The councillor wanted to know what had been the problem, and expressed concern about the impending gala. 'Do you know what caused the leak?' he asked.

'Not really, there was obviously a fault in the filtration system but the engineers couldn't find an actual leak. We are just hoping it won't all leak out again before Saturday.'

'Yes, that would be most unfortunate. We've got some very important people coming, as you know.'

'Yes, and of course the swimmers haven't been able to practice here. We arranged for them to go to Anderstown pool in the meantime.'

'Are they charging us for that?' the councillor asked.

'I hope not, I suggested that if they ever had a problem we would help them out.'

'That was very resourceful of you, well done.' He patted her on the back and smiled benignly.

The next stop was the Riverside Community Centre, where Mervyn was introduced to the manager and the two assistants who were organising a session of games for wheelchair users.

'I'd like you to take particular interest in this group, Davis,' said the councillor. 'Do everything you can for them. We've just had some disabled facilities installed at the West End Community Centre and I'd like to know what they think of them. Organise a meeting would you, and let me know what they say.'

The rest of the day was taken up with visits to more of the council's facilities and by the time the councillor bade him goodbye, Mervyn was tired and could remember very few of the names of the people he had met. He would have to ask George to make him a list.

4

Eager to please the councillor, who had shown such an interest in him, Mervyn asked George how he could get in touch with the disabled group he had seen at the community centre.

'The guy you want to talk to is Phil Stevens, nice chap; he fell off some scaffolding and broke his back. Can't walk now but he's a mean basketball player and he organises the disabled group. They are called the West End Wheelers. They're based at the West End Community Centre, that's why they've put disabled toilets and ramps in for them. Simon Short is the manager there, give him a ring and arrange a meeting,'

As it happened the disabled group was in that very morning so Mervyn drove over, having checked with George the best way to get there.

When he arrived he found one of the wheelchair users in heated conversation with a very tall man who Mervyn thought was probably Simon Short. He went over and introduced himself.

'Oh, good, the very man!' exclaimed the man in the wheelchair. 'My name is Phil Stevens, I run the West End Wheelers. Just come with me and see this!' He was obviously cross about something. Mervyn followed him, having to trot to keep up.

'Look at this!' said Phil, pointing at the sign on the toilet door. 'Disabled Toilet.'

Mervyn looked.

'Well, what do you see?' asked Phil, looking at Mervyn and expecting a response.'

'I'm very sorry – what is the problem?'

'Problem? Problem! Look at it!'

Mervyn opened the toilet door. Inside was a toilet with handles to help a disabled person manoeuvre, and a wash-basin, lower down than usual. There was a red bell-pull for emergency use and everything looked sparkling clean. He couldn't see anything wrong.

'Well?' said Phil.

'You'll have to tell me, I'm sorry.'

'I can't get in. Look.' He propelled himself to the door and tried to open it. The door opened outwards and when the wheelchair was near enough to allow the user to get hold of the handle it was impossible to open the door.

'Oh, I see. I'm sorry. I couldn't see what you were trying to tell me, but now of course I can. That's ridiculous. Didn't the architects consult with you before installing the toilets?'

'Clearly not. Do they ever? And that's not all. Come and see this.' He spun his chair round and sped off down the corridor, with Mervyn in pursuit. He caught up as Phil entered a room at the end of the corridor. A sign over the door announced that the emergency exit was this way.

'Look at this – the new emergency exit – for wheelchair users.' He leaned out of his chair and pushed open the door. A ramp led from the door onto a tarmac area adjacent to the car-park. Mervyn thought it looked very convenient. Phil was very agitated.

'I'm sorry Mr Stevens. You'll have to explain to me again.'

Phil sighed, 'There's a step up to the door this side. I can't get up it.'

'Oh, I see! Yes of course, I saw the ramp and thought that was good but if you can't get out of the door it is useless.'

'Precisely. So what are you going to do about it?' Phil demanded.

'I'll get onto the architects immediately. It will be sorted, I assure you. I'm sorry, Mr Stevens, I've only just started in this job and I didn't know about this. I will get it put right, you can depend on me.'

Phil looked calmer and took Mervyn's offered hand. 'OK, Mr Davis. I'll look forward to it. Thank you. Oh, I'm sorry I was a bit, well, you know.'

'That is perfectly all right and quite understandable in the circumstances. Nice to meet you. I'll be in touch very soon.'

Mervyn returned to his office where he quickly made notes about the disabled access and then asked George where he could find the architect's department. It was clear that if today was anything to go by the job of Liaison Officer was very much needed and would be in great demand.

5

Mervyn learned that the architects' department was on the top floor of the Town Hall, and rather than face the wrath of the traffic warden again, he decided to go by bus.

'Where can I get a bus to the Town Hall, George?'

'A bus? What do you want to go on a bus for?'

Mervyn explained the trouble he'd had before and said he thought it would be easier to use public transport.

'You don't want to do that, you won't get your expenses,' explained George. 'Tell you what, I'll drive you, or you can drive and I'll bring your car back here and then when you're ready I'll come and fetch you. I've nothing else on this morning.'

'That's very kind of you, George, but it does seem a bit extravagant, it means two journeys.'

'And two lots of miles. Don't forget that,' smiled George.

'Oh, go on then, just this once. Thanks, George.'

'I want to have a go in your new car,' said George taking his coat from the back of his chair. 'Do you want a cuppa before we go?'

'No, better get on.'
'Right Oh, Chief.'

Mervyn was greeted cordially by Harry, the doorman, and felt a comfortable glow of belonging as he took the lift to the top floor.

The Architects' Department was very different to the other departments Mervyn had seen so far. All the furniture looked new, the walls were covered in simulated suede and there was carpet on the floor. A very attractive young lady sat at a desk in the foyer. Mervyn approached.

'Good morning, my name is Mervyn Davis, I'm the Liaison Officer. Who do I need to speak to about disabled toilets?'

'That would be Mr Braithwaite, but have you got an appointment?'

'No, I haven't, but this is important.'

'Well, I don't think Mr Braithwaite will see you without an appointment, but I'll ask.'

She picked up a smart modernistic telephone handset and pressed a button on her console. 'Oh, Mr Braithwaite, I'm sorry, but there's someone here to see you, he says it is urgent. No, he doesn't have an appointment. No, he works at Hardcastle House. Very well.' The receptionist looked up at Mervyn, and smiled.' You're very honoured, he'll see you. If you would just wait a minute or two. Take a seat.'

Mervyn sat on one of an arrangement of four chairs next to a table covered with architectural magazines, some of which were in foreign languages. He picked up a glossy copy of *Architettura* and began flicking through its pages.

'Mr Davis?' asked a tall, immaculately dressed man, who had emerged from an adjacent office.

'Yes, that's me,' said Mervyn, standing and putting down the magazine.

The new arrival bent to straighten the magazine on the table then offered his hand to Mervyn. 'Braithwaite, how can I help?'

'I've been speaking to Phil Stevens – the . . .'

'Oh, him. You'd better come through.' He led the way into his office which was furnished in what might be described as minimalist décor. Everything was grey, the carpet, the walls, the chairs, even the desk. But although the palette was modest, the cost must have been quite the reverse.

'Have a seat, Mr Davis. You're new, I take it?'

'Yes, I only started this week. I'm finding my way round.'

'You started with a difficult customer, I'm afraid. He gives us a lot of grief.'

'Well, in this instance at least, I think, probably not without good cause.'

'Oh? Why is that?'

Mervyn explained the problem with the disabled toilet and the emergency exit ramp. 'Something will have to be done, or the disabled group won't be able to use the building.'

Mr Braithwaite was silent for a moment. 'I see, I see,' he said, then suddenly got up and came round to Mervyn's side of the desk, holding out his hand. 'Thank you for bringing this to my attention, Mr Davis. I'll see what can be done.' Mervyn was clearly being dismissed and allowed himself to be led to the door.

Before he know what had happened he found himself in the lift descending to ground level and reality.

Harry the doorman was standing by his cubby-hole when Mervyn got out of the lift. 'That was quick, did you get what you wanted?'

'I'm not sure. I'm really not sure. Would you do me a favour, Harry? Phone George for me and ask him to come and pick me up.'

George must have been waiting for the phone call as he took only about five minutes to get to the Town Hall. He parked in the Mayor's spot and ran up the steps to find Mervyn.

Mervyn began to tell George about his meeting with Mr Braithwaite while they were driving back to the office.

'I think you need a cuppa,' said George, as they got out of the car.'

'I think I do, George, Thanks.'

6

When Mervyn arrived at the office next morning, he found George looking very anxious.

'What's the problem, George?' he asked.

'Phone call, just now, the chief wanted to talk to you. I didn't know what to say as you weren't in yet. It's urgent, Mervyn, you need to phone him.'

'It's only just nine o'clock George, I'm not late. Who do you mean by the chief?'

'Chief exec. The big boss, he who must be obeyed. I don't know what you've done, but it must be serious if he wants to talk to you.'

'I'm sure it's nothing, George. What's his number?'

'One hundred on the internal. You'd better get on to him straight away.'

'What, even before we have a cuppa, George?' asked Mervyn, laughing.

'Yes, really, I mean it.'

Still smiling at George's anxiety, Mervyn dialled the number on the internal phone.

'It's Mervyn Davis here, you phoned. How can I help?'

'Duncan Macallister here, Chief Executive, we haven't met yet. You'd better get round here, Davis. I need to speak to you.'

'Oh, right oh then, do you mean now?'

'Yes, I do mean now. As soon as you can.' And with that the chief put down the phone, leaving Mervyn somewhat puzzled.

'Whatever do you think that was all about, George. He wants me to get round there now. Where does he hang out?'

'Did Councillor Matthews take you to the museum on your tour?'

'He pointed it out as we passed, but there wasn't time to go in. I hope to have a look round some time.'

'Yes, well, you'll see inside today. The Chief has his office there. Go in the front door and ask at reception.'

'Thanks, George, I'd better get off then, I'll see you later.'

'I hope so. Best of luck.'

Mervyn consulted his street map as he was not sure how to find the museum again. They had passed the impressive building on their way round, but he hadn't really noted where it was in relation to anything else they had seen. It was some time later when he found the entrance to the extensive grounds in which the museum was situated. He parked next to several other cars and went in.

The receptionist was expecting him and showed him the way to the Chief Executive's Suite.

'Just knock and go in, he's expecting you,' she said, smiling sweetly.

The Chief was sitting behind a desk the size of an aircraft carrier in a room furnished with antiques and hung with paintings; he stood when Mervyn entered.

'Ah, Davis,' he said and held out his hand. 'Come in, have a seat. Mervyn leaned across the desk and took the proffered hand and sat in the chair facing the big man.

'Now, Davis, you haven't been with us long have you? And yet you have already started upsetting people.'

'Oh, I was not aware that I had . . .' began Mervyn.

'Rupert Braithwaite, the Chief Architect, perhaps?'

'Oh, yes, I did see Mr Braithwaite but I didn't think I had upset him.'

'Well you did. He was on to me after you had been to see him. He said you had criticised his work. Is that not so?'

'I pointed out that the disabled toilets in the West End Community Centre were unfit for purpose, and that the disabled emergency exit ramp was inaccessible to someone in a wheelchair.'

'And you didn't think that was a criticism of his work?'

'Not as such. I just thought they might like to look at it again and perhaps make some alterations.'

'Mm. Well, if what you say is true, and the disabled facilities are not suitable, then you were right to bring it to the notice of the architects. However the correct procedure would be to inform your line manager. He would then approach the architects and mention that something might be amiss. You have to tread carefully with these people you see.' He paused, looking intently at Mervyn for a moment before going on. 'Leave it with me, Davis. I'll look into this myself and I'll get back to you. Don't worry, you did well. If you have any difficulties, just let my secretary know and I'll see what I can do.' He stood and smiled. Mervyn mumbled his thanks and left the room.

On his way out he waved to the receptionist and smiled. That was interesting, he thought. He had been expecting a rocket for some misdemeanour and it turned out to be a positive encounter. He already had two allies. And he had yet to meet his boss.

Back at William Hardcastle House, Mervyn told George about his meeting with the chief executive.

'He didn't tear you off a strip then?' asked George, incredulously.

'No, he was as nice as pie. Actually congratulated me on drawing his attention to the disabled loos at West End. He's going to look into it himself.'

'Wow, nice doing, you'll go far!' said George with a grin. 'Cuppa?'

'Please, and a cracker biscuit, I think.' Both men laughed and Mervyn sat at his desk, feeling that this job was going to be all right.

When George came back with the mugs of coffee and the ubiquitous packet of cracker biscuits, they sat munching in silence for several minutes before George suddenly jumped up. 'I've just remembered, the Amenities Committee is meeting tonight. You should go to that. It's at seven o'clock, here. Is that OK?'

'I haven't been invited,' said Mervyn.

'No, you wouldn't be, but you should be there. You'll be a key worker in the department. You'll get to meet all the important people.'

'Oh, right oh, George, thanks. Will you be there?'

'I just open up the building and make the tea. They don't usually want me in on the meeting.'

'If it's at seven I'd better get off early so I can get something to eat and change into a suit,' said Mervyn, shuffling a few papers on his desk.

'A suit?' asked George, with raised eyebrows.

'Well, yes if it's a committee meeting, don't people dress smart for these things?'

'You'll soon discover that with the number of committee meetings there are, there isn't time to change into a suit, or anything else. Just come as you are.'

The meeting of the Amenities Committee was as instructive as everything else had been so far. The chairman was Councillor Matthews, of course, and principal attendees were the police superintendent, the heads of the various departments; the managers of the swimming pool and the community centres and the museum curator, head teachers of two of the town's schools, along with the chairmen of their governing bodies. The chairman of the union of residents' associations and representatives from several residents' associations made up the numbers. They all appeared to know each other and Mervyn was barely noticed until Councillor Matthews called the meeting to order and introduced the new member of staff.

'I am sure Mervyn will make contact with you all in due course, but if in the meantime you need to speak to him you know where to find him,' the councillor began. 'Mervyn, on behalf of the Amenities Committee, welcome. And I think it is appropriate that you take the minutes of these meetings in future. Is that all right?'

'Oh, yes, that's fine. And thank you, Councillor.'

'Very well. You all have an agenda I think. But before we get on, I'd like to say that Mervyn has already make his mark by getting some action on the disabled facilities at West End, isn't that right, Anthony?' the councillor gestured to the manager of the community centre.

'That's right, Councillor. We were very impressed when the chief called to see for himself the bodged job that had been done on the toilets and the ramp. Very soon after that one of the architects came and the builders are going to start work on Monday putting it right. So, thank you very much, Mervyn, from me and the disabled group.'

Mervyn felt a warm glow from the smiles of all the committee members. He just hoped he would be able to keep it up.

The meeting ground on for nearly two hours in which he had a job keeping up with making notes. He had never taken minutes before and worried that he would miss something important. The only light relief in the meeting was when George wheeled in a trolley of tea and cakes.

After the meeting had been wound up, everyone wanted to talk to Mervyn about their own particular worries. He assured them all that he would attend to them and made notes of their names and telephone numbers. He was going to be very busy.

The first job the next morning was trying to make sense of the notes he had taken at the meeting. Trying to read his scribbled writing and remember what had been said was almost impossible.

'What am I going to do about these minutes, George,' he asked. 'I can't read my writing. I've no idea how to present a set of minutes. I've never done anything like this before. Don't they have a secretary for these things?'

'They used to, but the girl they had was hopeless, so they dismissed her. Mrs Cooper, one of the residents association people, took on the job after that. You could ask her, she might have taken her own notes.'

'Oh, good idea, George, thanks. Have we got her number?'

'It's in the book. Do you want a cuppa?'

While George made the coffee, Mervyn rang Mrs Cooper and asked if she had taken notes of the meeting. She had, and would be happy to compare if Mervyn would like to call round.

Mervyn hadn't really taken much notice of Mrs Cooper at the meeting, it had been so hectic. Now faced with her in her own territory, he found her a little frightening. She was a buxom middle-aged lady, with bleached blonde hair and rather too much make-up, dressed in a manner more suitable for a much younger woman, she had clearly taken some trouble to make herself look attractive for her guest.

'Come on in, Dear,' she cooed, ushering Mervyn into the tiny hallway of her neat council semi.

'Let me take your coat, you won't feel the benefit when you go out if you keep it on.'

Reluctantly, Mervyn took off his coat and allowed himself to be led into the fussily furnished sitting-room

'Would you like a cup of tea, or something stronger? I've got some sherry, or there's some beer, I think. I don't drink myself of course, but it's nice to have a drop in for visitors, don't you think?'

'No, really, I'm all right, thank you,' said Mervyn, not wanting to get bogged down. 'You said you had taken some notes of the meeting and I'm afraid my notes are a bit vague. I'm hoping you will be able to help me.'

'I'll be glad to, Dear. Sit yourself down and get comfortable. I'll just get my notepad.'

She scuttled away and returned with a large folder which she placed on the arm of her chair before sitting facing Mervyn.

'It's Molly, by the way, I know you are Mervyn, I hope you don't mind me calling you Mervyn, that's Welsh, isn't it? My Ronnie and me used to go to Colwyn Bay for our holidays, we loved it there. Ronnie is dead now, poor love. I'm all on my own. Are you married, Dear?'

After an hour and a half in which Molly had related most of her life story and details of the bed and breakfast in Colwyn Bay, as well as a little about the Amenities Committee meeting, Mervyn felt relieved to have got away with his virtue. He hurried back to the office to write up what he could about the meeting.

When Cyril Openthwaite finally returned from his long weekend, Mervyn already felt part of the Amenities Division team and he was able to talk to his new boss in terms they both understood.

Mr Openthwaite – there was to be no familiarity here – turned out to be a dapper little man, barely five foot four and almost as much round as he was tall. His suit could have been an exhibit in the museum. His hair was immaculately combed in such a way that it looked painted on, and his face was so smooth it was difficult to imagine whiskers ever sullying its surface. His office was furnished in a style to match the antiquity of the building. Everything was of an age. It was rather like a film set for a production of some Victorian drama.

Mervyn had been summoned, via George, to present himself at precisely ten o'clock, after George had taken in a cup – not a mug – of coffee, and a chocolate biscuit, on a tray. Mervyn was not invited to sit.

'So, tell me what you have been up to, Davis. I'm sorry I was not able to be here to greet you when you arrived. I trust Mr Conway has looked after you and shown you round?'

'Mr Conway?' asked Mervyn, momentarily confused. 'Oh, you mean George, yes he has, thank you.'

'I mean Mr Conway. I don't hold with all this Christian name nonsense. It doesn't command respect. You can call me Mr Openthwaite, or if that is too much of a mouthful for you – Sir. Is that understood?'

'Of course, Mr Openthwaite,' said Mervyn, who was not going to call anyone Sir if he could help it.

'I shall leave you to get on with your work and I don't tend to interfere, but I will want to know what you have been doing, so a written report each week will be sufficient. Anything you need in the way of information, of course, I will be happy to provide, but please do not keep bothering me with trivialities. I am far too busy. Now, will you send in Mr Conway. I have an errand for him. Thank you.'

Later, when Mervyn saw George in the photocopying room, he asked if he had done Mr Openthwaite's errand.

'I'm doing it now, he calls everything an errand, whether it's getting his cup of tea or going to Singh's for a newspaper. I'm photocopying a library book for him now.'

'What, all of it?' asked Mervyn, amazed at the growing pile of paper in the tray.

'Yes, he's giving a lecture in Manchester at the end of the week and he wants the pages in a form that he can refer to easily, rather than in a book.'

'But isn't that rather expensive?'

'You tell me,' said George, turning over another page of the thick book.

'How many pages is it?'

'Er, three hundred and fifty odd, I think.'

'What is it called, this book?'

'I'm not sure, hold on,' he turned the book over and read the title, '*Deliberations of Community Development in an Urban Context.* By some Russian geezer by the look of it, *Metzikov,* there you are, see?' he held the book up for Mervyn to see.

'Does he do a lot of lectures?'

'At least one a month. He seems to be quite popular. Can't think why, the stuff he has me copying sounds as dull as ditchwater.'

'Do you see much of him in the office?'

'Not a lot. He's out most of the time. Good job if you ask me. I can't get on when he's around.'

7

It was the night of the Mayor's New Year Ball. Held in Riverside, the largest of the community centres. It was the event of the year, to which almost everyone who was anyone was invited. All the department heads, principal officers and deputies, area managers and supervisors, along with all the most important people in the business sector of the town, the police commissioner, the managing directors of the big manufacturing companies, and the chairmen of the numerous charity organisations.

Mervyn was invited too. It was a dinner jacket occasion so he'd had to hire the appropriate outfit. He felt very uncomfortable as he made his entrance.

George – how would the council ever mange without him? – had been appointed as usher, and was doing a sterling job announcing people as they arrived. Who else knew absolutely everybody's name?

Mr Openthwaite was holding court, in the centre of the room. He was talking loudly to the police commissioner, resplendent in dress uniform. When he spotted Mervyn he raised a finger and an eyebrow. Mervyn went over.

'How do you do? Mr Davis, isn't it?' said the policeman, holding out his hand.

'Yes, that's right, how do you do?'

'William Meadows, I'm very pleased to meet you.'

'That's Commissioner Meadows, Davis,' Mr Openthwaite said, emphasising the policeman's rank.

'Yes, that's right, Cyril, but let's not be formal. We're all friends aren't we?' said the policeman, smiling.

Mr Openthwaite said nothing, clearly not happy to be anyone's friend.

Fortunately, just then the band began to play and all conversation was drowned. Mervyn took a glass from a passing tray and turned to face the stage where the band was playing the town's signature tune.

The music faded and the Mayor, in all his finery, took the centre spot on the stage. He held up his hands for attention and the room fell silent.

The mayor spoke for several minutes and afterwards Mervyn couldn't have told you what he talked about, but it didn't matter, the mood was positive, everyone was having a good time and the food and drink was plentiful. The mayor was everyone's hero, for now at least.

Cyril Openthwaite was making sure he spoke to all the most important people, at the same time as keeping his eye on his staff to make sure they behaved appropriately. At one point he waved to Mervyn, urgently beckoning him over to his table. Mervyn dutifully presented himself and adopted a posture that he hoped said 'Yes, can I help?' the music was so loud he couldn't have heard himself speak. Mr Openthwaite gestured towards the table where the mayor sat alone. He shouted in Mervyn's ear, 'There's nobody talking to the mayor! Go and talk to him!'

'Me?' gestured Mervyn.

'Yes, go on!' shouted Openthwaite.

Unsure why his boss was so keen for him to speak to the mayor, he nevertheless made his way to the mayor's table.

'Good evening, Mr Mayor. It is a wonderful evening. Thank you so much for inviting me,' he said, unsure how he should address a person of such high rank.

'That's nice of you, son. You're the only person who has thanked me. But actually I don't do the inviting. It's all done by my secretary. I don't even know most of the people here. Who are you?'

'I'm new to the council, I only started a month ago. My name is Mervyn Davis, I'm the Liaison Officer for the Amenities Division.'

'Oh, Councillor Matthews' new boy. How is it going?'

'Very well, thank you, and I'm enjoying it.'

'I'm so pleased. Councillor Matthews had a job getting it through council but I thought it sounded a good idea. I wonder if you would be so good as to keep me posted how you get on. Say once a month, you could come and have a coffee with me and tell me what's happening. I only get to read boring reports that come from departmental heads and I'm sure they only write what they think I want to see, rather than what is actually happening. Will you do that?'

'Of course, I'll be glad to,' said Mervyn, wondering what he had got himself into.

'Off you go now, son, enjoy yourself.' The mayor smiled and did a little mock salute as Mervyn melted into the crowd. He looked round and not seeing anyone he knew, decided he'd had enough and quietly left. He didn't say goodbye to anyone.

The following Monday morning Mr Openthwaite was early for once and asked George to call Mervyn in to his office.

'What were you talking to the mayor about on Saturday?'

'Well, you told me to talk to him, just small talk you know. I thanked him for inviting me and said it was a good do.'

'You have to be careful what you say to the mayor you know,' cautioned Mr Openthwaite, and Mervyn nodded, as if he understood perfectly. 'Very well, off you go. Tell Mr Conway to come in.'

Later, while they were drinking their first mug coffee, George asked the same question. Evidently several people had seen Mervyn talking to the mayor and they all wanted to know what he was saying. For some reason Mervyn didn't feel he should tell anyone about the mayor's request. He would keep it to himself. For now at least.

8

By Easter, Mervyn had settled into a routine as much as was possible. He could find his way round the town most of the time without using his street map. He had made some very useful allies, Councillor Matthews of course, the Mayor, with whom he had a weekly meeting over tea and cakes in the Mayor's Parlour, and most of the managers of the community centres. However, he had adversaries too. Not enemies, that was too strong, but people who could and did make things very difficult for him. The worst of these was his own boss, Cyril Openthwaite, who it seemed, had taken a dislike to Mervyn and was always sniping at him over some real or imaginary fault or omission. He had accused Mervyn of neglecting Health and Safety Regulations, falsifying his expenses – this was something that everyone was accused of at least once a year – and, of all things, toadying to the Councillors and especially the

Mayor himself. This to Mr Openthwaite was a crime akin to treason. The only thing Mervyn could do was keep out of Mr Openthwaite's way as much as possible. Fortunately, Mr Openthwaite was away quite a lot, and George would let Mervyn know when the coast was clear. On these occasions he was able to join George for coffee and cracker biscuits in his office. But he spent most of his time in the various establishments that most needed his assistance, such as the community centres and especially the swimming pool, where he enjoyed talking to Vanessa, the attractive young receptionist.

Evenings were taken up by the many residents' associations, all of which, it seemed, had been waiting for someone like Mervyn to sort out their troubles. Most of the complaints came from council house tenants whose houses were in need of repair. The council was responsible for the maintenance of the houses but fell short of expectations in a big way. The maintenance team were hard pressed to keep up with repairs and the men who had been given the job of replacing outdated kitchens in a rash moment of generosity by a previous council, just could not keep up with demand.

Mervyn was expected to be able to solve all the problems and it was difficult for him to explain that he didn't have a pot of money at his disposal for repairs and improvements.

When he approached one of the schools with a view to attending their governors' meeting as an observer, the head teacher was overjoyed when he explained who he was.

'Man from the Council? Of course you can. Would you like to be a governor?' was the excited response. It was pretty much the same wherever he went, and even when he explained that he wasn't necessarily going to be able to solve any problems at all, and could really only take back their complaints to the appropriate department, they still wanted him to be at the meetings.

One of the residents' associations had invited Mervyn to their meeting which was to be held in one of the tower blocks near to the one where Mervyn himself lived. He walked the short distance across the grass and looked for the lift that called at the odd numbers. The towers were fifteen floors high, and two lifts were provided, one for even numbered floors and one for odds. Often one of the lifts was out of order and then you would have to go to the next adjacent floor and either climb or descend the stairs, depending how energetic you were feeling. Once, both lifts in Mervyn's tower had been out of order at the same time and he'd had to climb all the way to his flat on the top floor by the stairs.

A young man, dressed in jeans and motor-cycle leather jacket, came and stood by Mervyn. 'Called it, 'ave yer?' he said amiably.

'Yes, I think I can hear it coming.'

'I haven't seen you before, do you live here?' the young man asked.

'No, I live in Wilson Tower, I'm just visiting. Going to a committee meeting actually.'

'Oh, residents' meeting is it?'

'Yes, that's right.'

'Me too. Tony Purbright, how are you?' He held out his hand.

'Good to meet you, Tony, Mervyn Davis, I'm the council liaison officer.'

'Oh right. They've asked you to come have they? They said they would, as soon as we heard there was going to be a you.'

'Be a you?' asked Mervyn.

'Yes, as soon as they knew there was going to be liaison bloke.'

'Oh, I see, of course.'

'Quite a few problems want sorting out, you see. The council hasn't been very helpful up to now. We are hoping you'll be able to help us.'

'That's what they all say. I can't always help though. It rather depends what it is.'

'You'll see in a bit – have you brought a notebook, there's quite a list.' He grinned impishly.

Mervyn was greeted enthusiastically by the members of the committee and he was quickly appraised of the many and various concerns of the residents. It seemed they had been complaining to the council about several outstanding problems for a very long time. Most often they didn't know to whom their complaints should be addressed and, as a result, most of them went unanswered.

Mervyn tried to explain that if they were unsure to whom they should address a concern, their local councillor would be able to help.

'Mm, not so's you'd notice,' harrumphed a man sitting in an easy chair, away from the table.

'Sh, Dad, don't say that,' said the large, fierce looking lady who was hosting the meeting.

'So, am I to understand that you have approached your councillor and he hasn't helped?' asked Mervyn.

'I'm afraid so, he's amiable enough, always says 'hello' if you see him in the street, but I'm not sure he even goes to Council meetings.'

'We won't be voting for him next time, that's for sure,' said another lady, as she came into the room bearing a tray of cups and a large teapot.

'I think you'd better tell me what your concerns are and I'll see what I can do,' said Mervyn, getting out his notebook.

The committee members introduced themselves and they settled down to drinking their tea and eating home-made biscuits before reading the minutes of the last meeting, which consisted mainly of a list of complaints ranging from problems with plumbing, power cuts, and refuse collection to rowdy youths congregating in the stairwells and lifts. Mervyn noted them all in his book.

Addressing the chairman, who he now knew to be called Adrian Bullen, Mervyn asked for the problems to be explained in detail. Adrian started to explain but was interrupted by the others who all seemed to have a different take on the problem.

Tony Purbright banged the table, 'Mr Chairman, may I say something?'

'Of course, Tony,' said Adrian, 'what is it?'

'Well, we'll never get anywhere like this, will we? Mervyn only lives in the next tower. Why don't I go over to his flat and tell him all our troubles quietly? What do you say, Mr Davis?'

'That sounds like a very good idea, Tony, I'd be glad to meet you in my flat. Then you can get on with your meeting without having to go over old ground, as it were.'

'Yes, well, most of the meetings are usually about the problems we have, but I can see it would be easier for you if just one of us explains. Does everyone agree?' asked Adrian.

There were mumblings of assent and Mervyn arranged a time for Tony to come to see him, then bade everyone goodnight. He was pleased to be able to get away.

On his way back to his flat Mervyn saw for himself the groups of youths hanging out in the stairwells. Most of them seemed to be smoking and, judging from the strong smell of bonfires, it was not necessarily tobacco they were smoking. Some had cans of lager and although they were not threatening in any way, Mervyn could see that elderly people and women on their own might well feel uncomfortable having to go through the crowd on their way home.

Mervyn nodded to the crowd and edged through to the lift and pressed the bell call button. He stood quietly, not making eye contact with any of the youths and when the lift arrived he entered it and pressed the button for his floor. He turned as the doors closed and said 'Night, lads.' Much to his surprise, several of the boys answered, 'Night, Mister.' Mervyn resolved to try talking to the boys next time he saw them.

The view of the town from the fifteenth floor was spectacular. Everything was lit with orange street-lights, and the traffic lights and lights on vehicles made a sort of kaleidoscope. Most of the time little could be heard from below but occasionally the sound of a police car or ambulance siren would come eerily up to Mervyn's level. He stood for quite a long time thinking about all the people he had met and their many and diverse problems.

9

Mervyn's meeting with the boys in the stairwell came much sooner than he had anticipated. The next evening he had to go to a meeting of managers at the Museum. The Chief Executive wanted to tell the staff about an idea he had come across on a visit to Sweden and as his office was in the Museum it seemed a good place to meet. It also had the advantage of a very good catering department, so refreshments were provided. The idea was for 'One Stop Shops', places where members of the public could access services and information and, of course, lodge complaints. The response was mixed. Many of the managers said that the public was well able to complain already without it being made easier, but others were quite amenable. If the idea was to go ahead Mervyn would be put in charge as he was already doing much of the work that such a facility would provide.

Mervyn was quite preoccupied when he reached Wilson Tower and merely nodded to the group of youths he had seen before, but then, just as he was about to get into the lift, he remembered that he had decided to talk to the youngsters. He turned to them and smiled.

'Hello, Mister, all right?' said one of the lads.

'Hello, yes, how are you? Have you nowhere you can meet where it's a bit more comfortable than this draughty old stairwell?'

'Nobody'll have us,' said another boy.

'The community centres won't let us in, we're too young for the pub and there's no youth club. At least not for us.'

The youths went on to explain that the community centres would not let them in unless they were enrolled in a specific activity and, apart from the fact that they could not afford the fees, there really wasn't anything they wanted to join. They would have liked a game of table tennis or badminton, and they would have loved to use the snooker table, but although there were clubs for these activities they just wanted to play casually, now and again, as the whim took them. What they needed, Mervyn realised, was a youth club. Why were there no youth clubs? He would ask.

'Look boys, leave this with me. I'll find out why you can't use the centres, but you really need somewhere of your own to hang out.'

Mervyn thought he would ask George about the lack of youth clubs before bringing it up with anyone else.

'The community centre managers can't be bothered with the youngsters – that's the top and bottom of it, rather than there being a specific policy,' explained George, next morning over coffee and cracker biscuits.

'But hasn't anyone raised it – I mean, these youngsters are always being criticised for hanging round the stairwells of the flats and so on, but if they've nowhere else to go, what are they to do?'

Mervyn decided to mention it to the mayor next time he saw him. He was determined to do something for these young people.

The mayor was sympathetic, but didn't have any suggestions. 'Talk to Councillor Matthews, my boy, see what he thinks.'

Councillor Matthews agreed with Mervyn that something needed to be done about the youths hanging round the stairwells but didn't think he would be able to force the community centre managers to allow the youngsters into the centres. The other users would complain or stop using the centres themselves, and as the council relied on the fees that regular users paid, that wouldn't do at all.

'Have there never been proper youth clubs in the town?' Mervyn wanted to know.

'Well there are youth clubs you know, proper organised ones . . .'

'Well, why doesn't anybody seem to know about them?'

After asking a lot of people Mervyn finally tracked down someone who knew about the alleged youth clubs. It turned out that they were nothing more than after school activity clubs that had been given the misleading name youth clubs to get round the obligation to provide facilities for young people. They catered for children aged from about eight to twelve and were held in some of the community centres between four and six in the afternoon, before the main business of the centres got under way. They had paid leaders, most of them school teachers, and the activities were designed to use up as much energy as possible with as little imagination on the part of the leaders as possible. Mervyn was not impressed. He went back to Councillor Matthews.

'I would really like to do something about this, Councillor,' he began, when they met over a pint one evening. 'But I don't know how to. I don't know who I should talk to, nobody really seems interested. I really need your help with this one.'

'I suggest you find out if there are any redundant buildings that you might use. The architects' department would know about them, if there are any,' suggested the councillor.

Mervyn didn't fancy another foray into the architects' department but he was not going to be deterred. This time he made sure he had an appointment, to see one of the junior architects, who could spare him a few minutes.

'You really need the works department I suppose, but we do have a list of buildings that are ripe for development. That might be useful,' the sharply dressed young hopeful explained.

'What sort of buildings are they?' asked Mervyn.

'There are all sorts as I recall, everything from public toilets to an old gunpowder factory.'

'Can I see them?' asked Mervyn.

'Well, I would have to get approval from my department chief, but I suppose something could be arranged. I'll see if I can get hold of the list, then perhaps we could filter out a few possibilities.'

'That sounds splendid,' said Mervyn, 'can I see the list now?'

'Oh, well, that might be difficult. Leave it with me and I'll get back to you,' said the young man.

10

Somewhat to Mervyn's surprise, Robin, the young architect, telephoned soon after Mervyn arrived in the office on Monday morning.

'Mr Davis? It's Robin Stroud, architects' department . . .'

'Yes, hello, Mr Stroud, thank you for getting back to me. Any luck?'

'Yes, actually, I think you will be pleased. I have a list of buildings that might be useful. Perhaps we could meet and go through them?'

'That would be splendid. Shall I come to your office?'

'No! Er, no, sorry, no, don't do that. I'll, er, come to yours if you like. I know where you are. Would later this morning be convenient?'

'Indeed it would, any time this morning in fact. I'll look forward to seeing you.'

Mervyn put down the phone and looked across the desk at George, who was agog to know what was being arranged. Mervyn suggested a cup of coffee and a biscuit and he would tell all.

George was very impressed when Mervyn explained that he had got one of the architects to cooperate. They were well known for being awkward and unhelpful.

Robin Stroud arrived at eleven o'clock, just in time for coffee. It wouldn't have mattered what time he arrived in fact, it would have been in time for coffee any time, morning or afternoon. Thinking that perhaps cracker biscuits were something of an acquired taste, Mervyn had asked George to go across the road to Singh's Emporium for some decent biscuits for their guest, and he had found some reasonable looking mugs for coffee.

The list of properties included, as Robin had said, a public toilet and a disused gunpowder factory, but it was the sports pavilion that caught Mervyn's eye.

'Why isn't it still used as a sports pavilion?' Mervyn wanted to know.

'The field is no longer used for football I understand, and a new pavilion has been built over by the new sports complex. The old pavilion has fallen into disrepair and there has been some vandalism, so . . .'

'Can we go and see it?' asked Mervyn, trying not to sound too eager.

The pavilion was a squat ugly building with grey cement rendering liberally covered with obscene graffiti. It stood on the edge of a public playing field which, judging from the tussocky, ill-kempt grass, was not used for much other than unauthorised grass-track bicycle racing. A circle of worn grass indicated the circuit and there were also car and motor bike tracks over most of the remainder of the field.

'It's ideal!' exclaimed Mervyn as soon as they got out of the car. This was an area obviously used by young people so if the pavilion could be converted it would be a natural meeting place.

'Oh, do you think so?' said Robin. 'I was afraid you would be disappointed.'

'Not at all. Do you think these changing rooms could be knocked into one to make a room for games – table tennis, maybe a snooker table and so on?' asked Mervyn.

'Yes, I'm sure, and there is already an area that would make a kitchen and you could have a bar for coffee and coke.' The young architect was getting quite enthusiastic and Mervyn could see him mentally redesigning the interior of the building.

'What would be the procedure for getting the building converted?' asked Mervyn.

'Oh, that I couldn't help you with. I should think you would have to get it through the council and if there was any money available they might approve the work.'

'Is that a possibility, would you say – on past experience?'

Robin didn't know much about council procedures and he had no experience to compare. He suggested that Mervyn speak to his line manager. Mervyn would have preferred to go back to Councillor Matthews but remembered the warning of his boss, to let him know what he was doing before going any further with his plans.

Cyril Openthwaite was not opposed to Mervyn's idea in principle, but warned that anything as radical as the introduction of a proper youth club was going to be difficult to get through council. He offered to talk to councillors himself in the first instance. Mervyn suspected that he would then be able to claim the idea as his own. He didn't mind, as long as the council was in favour. He felt very strongly that this should be done.

Mervyn had already learned that things in local government happen very slowly if at all, so was not surprised to be told that his idea would not be raised at the next session of the council. 'Be patient, Davis,' was the advice offered by Mr Openthwaite.

Despite his boss's advice, Mervyn did talk to Councillor Matthews the next time he saw him.

Councillor Matthews told Mervyn that he had heard a rumour among fellow councillors that Cyril Openthwaite had suggested the formation of a Borough Youth Service. The Councillor knew the idea had come from Mervyn and others suspected as much. Openthwaite was not known for innovation.

'You mustn't be too disappointed if your ideas are poached; it happens all the time. Just be pleased that the idea was good enough for Openthwaite to want to steal it. I'll see what I can do – I have some influential friends.' He smiled, conspiratorially and tapped the side of his nose.

In fact there was no further mention of Mervyn's idea for such a long time that he had almost forgotten it, and other things occupied his mind.

It was the season of Summer Shows. Each of the Borough's parliamentary wards put on a show each summer and they all tried very hard to put on the best possible event. Committees met all year round, planning and scheming. There had been some very extravagant attractions; hot air balloons, helicopter rides, Wild West displays, historic battle enactments, donkey derbies, and even one year, an air-show. This had been the highlight of the year's shows and people still talked about it, but it had been so expensive that it was unlikely to be repeated.

Mervyn was expected to oversee the entire program and had to attend many Show Committee meetings. One such was at the Riverside Community Centre, the biggest and proudest of them all. They felt honour bound to put on the best show, and the strain was showing.

All the most important local people seemed to be on the committee and they all wanted their say. Mervyn had been elected chairman as he was supposed to be impartial and he was having a tough time keeping everyone in check.

'I have put a lot of money into this event since the shows started in nineteen . . .'

'Yes, yes, we know, you tell us every year, Mr Smallbone. That doesn't give you the right to bulldoze your ideas to the top of the list,' interrupted a large redheaded woman, who Mervyn couldn't place. He leaned to whisper to the person sitting beside him.

'Who are they? The people arguing?' he asked.

'That's Albert Smallbone, he owns the big department store in the centre of town, Smallbone and Winterbourne. It's a very well established firm. Been in the town for generations. The woman is Agnes Whittle, the head teacher of Kingscourt Primary School.

She gets her nose into everything. Mind you, it is a very good school. People have been known to move house in order to get their kids into the catchment area.

The two were still arguing and Mervyn tried to bring them to order. 'Why don't we just make a list of everybody's ideas and see what it looks like,' he suggested.

After a while the meeting settled down and the semblance of a programme began to emerge. By the time they had finished, Mervyn was exhausted. The centre caretaker, Algernon Brown, had rattled his keys several times before everyone had left the building.

'I'm sorry, Mr Brown. I didn't do a very good job of keeping them to the agenda. I hope we haven't kept you too long.'

'That's OK, I'm used to it. Call me Algy by the way.'

'OK, Algy, I'm Mervyn.'

'I've got a brew on – do you fancy a cuppa before you go? I got fed up waiting so I thought I'd earned a break before I start tidying up for the morning.'

'That's very civil, Algy. Yes, I'd love a cuppa.'

By the time they had drunk their tea and had a long and interesting chat about things that had happened in the centre over the years, it was past midnight. If I got paid overtime, Mervyn thought to himself, I'd be a rich man.

11

Mervyn woke early to the sound of torrential rain. It was the morning of the first Summer Show which was being held at the Riverside Community Centre's sports field. He groaned, at the prospect of a washed out show and at the very idea of the show. He had attended so many meetings planning the shows that the arrangements had merged into one nightmarish event. He had dreamed about summer shows, and dreaded the very thought of them. Now the first was due to begin in less than six hours and it was raining. He desperately tried to think what arrangements had been made in case of rain. There was nothing he could do, but somehow he feared he would be blamed. Just lately everything had been going wrong. Last week, George, that pillar of reliability and common sense, the fount of knowledge and general dogsbody, had been accused of false accounting and fraudulent claims on his travelling expenses.

He had been suspended from duty pending an investigation and Mervyn had been left holding the fort. Everyone was aware that George knew the workings of the council better than anyone else, but nobody knew just how much George was responsible for – how many people relied on George for vital information, how much of the council's infrastructure depended upon George's knowledge and how many people's palms were greased by George to ensure the smooth running of just about everything. It was George that ordered fuel for the central heating in all the community centres and the swimming pool. It was George who made sure the coffee machines were kept filled. It was George who ordered milk for the councillors' tea. The list went on and on. And George hadn't written any of it down anywhere. He knew when to reorder and from whom and just did it. Mervyn had been forbidden from contacting George; he was *persona non grata* until such time as the accusations against him had been proved or disproved. Mervyn was the Liaison Officer so it was his responsibility to ensure that everything functioned properly.

Things had started to go wrong very quickly. The phone rang incessantly with irate people wanting to know why something or other had not happened. Where was the list of old people and their addresses who were picked up each day to go to the various community centres? And why wasn't there a bus to pick them up? Most pressing of all, today was the first, the biggest and most prestigious of all the shows and Mervyn couldn't remember even which celebrity had been invited to open it. Mervyn had tried to contact the illusive head of his department, the mysterious Cyril Openthwaite, but as usual he was nowhere to be found.

Mervyn realised that despite being warned not to contact George, it was the only solution open to him. So where did George live? Cyril would know, but he wasn't there to ask. Human Resources knew but he couldn't ask them as it was them that had issued the instruction to keep away from George. Vanessa from the swimming pool seemed to know George pretty well – would she know?

'Hello, could I speak to Vanessa, please, this is Mervyn Davis - Liaison Officer.'

Mervyn gripped the handset as if his life depended on it, and on reflection he realised that it probably did. If Vanessa didn't know where George lived he didn't know who else to ask . . . 'Hello, yes, Mervyn Davis, that's right.'

'She's not here at the moment, Mr Davis,' said the voice on the phone, 'She's gone to Huddersfield with a children's swimming team. They have a competition up there at the weekend. She won't be back until Monday. Right oh, then. Bye'

'That's it then, I might as well hand in my resignation now,' Mervyn said to himself as he put the phone down.

He spotted the battered internal telephone numbers book on George's desk and grabbed it eagerly.

'There must be someone in here that knows George well enough to know where he lives,' Mervyn said, again to himself. He flipped through the pages, desperately looking for a name he recognised. 'Hardeep, Hardeep, what was his surname?' He looked for Asian names – there were dozens – but none had the first name Hardeep. By chance he spotted Maintenance, George had listed Hardeep's number under Maintenance. Oh, Thank you, George.'

He dialled the number. 'Can I speak to Hardeep, please, yes, I'll wait.' He waited and eventually Hardeep came on the line.

'Hello, sorry, just having my tea break. What can I do for you, we're pretty busy just now.'

'Mervyn Davis here, Liaison . . .'

'Oh, hello, Mervyn, how are you? How's George?'

Mervyn explained as quickly as he could the situation with George and asked if Hardeep knew George's address.

'I think he lives in Newtown somewhere, one of the council estates along by the canal. I know he drinks in the Anvil and Hammer, that's by the locks, do you know it?'

'I think so, thank you, Hardeep, I'll try there. Thanks again. Bye.'

At last he was getting somewhere. He locked up the office and consulted the street-map in his car. Newtown, an area to the north of the town that had been extensively redeveloped in the nineteen sixties, was a maze of streets named after well known Labour members of parliament. The public house - The Anvil and Hammer was marked on the map, right next to one of the canal locks as Hardeep had said it was. It took Mervyn no more than fifteen minutes to find the pub and he parked next to a battered Ford Mondeo that hadn't seen a wash for many moons.

When Mervyn pushed open the door to the saloon, everything went quiet. The half dozen or so drinkers stopped in mid conversation and looked at Mervyn. The room was quite dark after the daylight outside, one might even say it was gloomy. Mervyn walked over to the bar where the barman stood holding a glass and a grubby tea-towel, looking less than friendly.

'Good afternoon, I wonder if you can help me?' he began. The expression on the barman's face did not change, but he went on, 'I need to contact George . . .' Mervyn suddenly realised he couldn't remember George's surname, he'd heard it once, from Cyril Openthwaite, but as everybody used first names it hadn't registered. 'George, who works for the council, I believe he drinks here.'

'What do want with George?' asked the barman, still looking unfriendly.

'I work with George and . . .'

'You work with George?'

'Yes, my name is Mervyn . . .'

'Oh, you're Mervyn, George talks about you,' said the barman with a huge grin that transformed his face. 'What can I get you to drink?'

'Oh, well, I didn't, I mean, well, Thank you, I'll have a pint of bitter then.'

Rather taken aback by the change in the barman's demeanour, Mervyn forgot for a moment what he had come in for and took the offered pint gratefully.

'That's two pound seventy-five,' said the grinning barman.

Mervyn paid him and then remembered his errand. 'Do you know where George lives, I need to speak to him rather urgently.'

Before Mervyn had a chance to taste his beer, all the men had crowded round offering to show him where George lived. They didn't know the address but they knew the house well enough as they had all, at some time, helped George home after a heavy night.

Having paid for his pint, Mervyn was determined to enjoy it before accepting the offer to show him George's house so it was fifteen minutes later when he walked up to the front door of a house that looked remarkably like several hundred others on the estate. A collection of broken-down motorcycles stood in various attitudes of disarray in George's front garden and what little grass there was on the lawn had not been blessed with the attention of a lawnmower for a very long time.

When Mervyn knocked, a curtain twitched in the window of the house next door but there was no response from George's door.

'E's gone out with 'is dog,' shouted a man from his garden across the road. 'Down by the canal.'

'Oh, thank you,' shouted Mervyn. 'How long ago did he go?'

''Ow should I know?' shouted the man.

'Well, how do you know that's where he's gone?'

''E always goes down the canal with 'is dog in the afternoon. That's 'ow.'

There seemed only one course of action available to Mervyn and he crossed the road and headed for the canal towpath. Not knowing how long George had been gone meant that the chances of catching up with him were pretty remote but he had to try.

The towpath, sadly no longer used for its original purpose since the canal wasn't used for the transport of heavy and bulky goods, was a very popular place to walk one's dog or simply oneself. A narrow strip of countryside threaded through an industrial landscape, it offered an escape from the town without having to travel too far. Today, Mervyn was too intent on finding George to notice the beauties of nature. Choosing the direction away from town, he hurried along as fast as his legs would carry him, barely noticing the puddles that the rain had produced.

In the distance Mervyn could just make out a group of people and dogs. Hoping against hope that George was among them he quickened his pace. Yes, George was there with his little dog, Speckle, talking to an elderly couple with a King Charles spaniel.

'George!' Mervyn called, while still twenty yards away. 'Hi, George!'

'Hello, Mervyn!' exclaimed George as Mervyn joined the little group. 'How are you? What are you doing up here?'

'I'm looking for you, George, I need your help.'

George turned to his companions, 'This is Mervyn, we work, or I should say, we used to work together. Mervyn, this is Ambrose and

Dorothy Williams, they both used to work for the council. They're retired now of course.'

'How do you do?' said Mervyn, offering his hand. 'Nice to meet you. Please forgive me for interrupting your conversation. I do need to talk to George rather urgently.'

They assured Mervyn that it was perfectly all right and that they were on the point of continuing their walk anyway. They bade George and Speckle goodbye and walked on. George turned to Mervyn.

'I'm not supposed to talk to anyone from the council, you know,' he said with a mischievous twinkle in his eye.

'No, I know, but this is important. You've got to help me George. I can't manage without you. Do you think we can clear up this nonsense and get you reinstated?'

'Nothing would please me more, Mervyn, as I'm sure you must know, but they have got it into their silly heads that I'm fiddling the books. I don't know what I can do. What's your problem anyway? I thought you were doing very well.'

'I can manage the meetings and most of the problems but there is so much that only you know about and I am out of my depth. The department is floundering, George, I desperately need you back there. Most important today is the show at Riverside. It starts in a couple of hours and if this rain persists I don't know what arrangements have been made and I don't remember who is opening the proceedings or where he or she is being met – I can't do it without you, George. You are going to have to come back.'

George could see how desperate Mervyn was but his instructions were clear – he must have no contact with anyone from the council until after the hearing. If he did make contact, both he and the person he contacted would be in serious trouble.

'I don't see what I can do, Mervyn. They'll have my job – and yours, I daresay.'

'Well how about if you hide in the office where I can ask you for information. Nobody is likely to find you there surely.'

'I'm not sure about that. The person opening the show is Morris Gantwich, from that telly programme about unusual sports. He's very popular with the youngsters, so I thought he'd be a good one to have.'

Mervyn didn't know the programme and had never heard of Morris Gantwich. 'I won't know him if I see him, George. How can I welcome him. Where am I supposed to meet him? Is he coming by train or car?'

'I see that could be a problem . . .' mused George, absentmindedly stroking Speckle's ears. 'Tell you what – I'll get my wife to come with you. She knows Gantwich so she'll be able to point him out to you.

George had never mentioned his wife to Mervyn who had assumed George was single.

'That would be super, George, can we get her now? The show is due to start any time. And what are the arrangements in case of rain?'

'We use the sports hall at Round Hill. It isn't far from the Riverside playing field and people will know that is the arrangement. We've only been rained off a couple of times but it is a well known alternative venue. Don't worry, they'll be ready for us if necessary.' George laid a comforting hand on Mervyn's arm and smiled. 'It'll be all right, you'll see.'

12

With George's wife, Jackie sitting in his car, armed with a mobile phone connected to George at home, ready to answer any questions, Mervyn felt better equipped to face the show. The sun had come out, just in time to prevent moving everything to the sports hall, and the people had come in their thousands – at least Mervyn thought there were thousands, a more realistic estimate might have been as many as five hundred, at any rate there were enough to make the show a success.

Jackie had been able to meet and greet the television personality who would open the show officially and he had been introduced to Mervyn and to the Mayor and his wife. Everything was going well, stalls and sideshows were doing a roaring trade and the events had been lined up, ready to perform in the arena. First on the bill was a display of acrobatic motor-cyclists and the screams and shouts from the crowd suggested it was being well received. Mervyn felt he could relax for a few minutes so he queued at an ice-cream van with a group of exited young children. Just as he was about to ask for a chocolate cornet, the wail of a police-car's siren made him hesitate. He looked round to see what was happening just in time to see three jam-sandwich police cars, sirens blaring, swoop into the showground. About a dozen policemen got out of the cars and ran towards the band-stand.

'Sorry, forget the ice-cream, I'd better see what's amiss,' he said to the ice-cream man, and then headed towards the bandstand.

'The police had surrounded the band-stand by the time Mervyn reached it. He saw a policeman he recognised from one of the committees and asked what was going on.

'Drugs,' said the policeman. 'We've been tipped off that members of the band are selling drugs in between numbers.'

'Who tipped you off?' asked Mervyn, horrified at the thought.

'We've had trouble with this group before, every time they do a gig, drugs are sold. We've never been able to prove anything, but this time I think we've got them red-handed.'

The music stopped and a few minutes later the five members of the group were led away in handcuffs, protesting loudly.

News of the arrests quickly spread throughout the crowd and people gathered round to see the band led away. It was the biggest excitement of the afternoon so far.

Anxious to keep the show going Mervyn asked the commentator to announce the next event – a display of falconry. Gradually the crowds made their way to the arena and order prevailed once more. Some enterprising member of the Riverside Community Centre staff had managed to rig up some recorded music and it was almost as if nothing had happened.

The rest of the afternoon passed without mishap, but by the end Mervyn was exhausted. The Mayor came over and congratulated the Riverside staff and Mervyn on a first class event and Councillor Matthews patted Mervyn on the back. 'Come and see me tomorrow,' he said, before disappearing into the departing crowd.

Mervyn took Jackie home to George and thanked them for their help. 'Do you know anything about the band, George? Have you heard that the police suspected them of drug dealing?'

'I had heard something about it, but as they were never charged I assumed it was OK to book them. They are very popular with the kids.'

'We shall have to be very careful who we book in future, George. It could have been disastrous today. I'm going to see Councillor Matthews tomorrow for a debriefing on the show and I'll see what I can do to get you reinstated.'

'Oh, thanks, Mervyn, but I don't think you'll have any joy. Once they accuse you of anything dodgy involving money, you've pretty much had it. I've seen it before. No, I'm afraid my days with the council are numbered.'

'Don't despair, George, when I tell Matthews how helpful you have been he'll have to do something.'

The meeting with Councillor Matthews was tense. He wanted to know all about the police raid and why the group hadn't been vetted properly. Mervyn then had the opportunity to explain how much George was involved in pretty much everything that happened in the division and how they really couldn't do without him.

'But isn't he suspended pending an investigation – false accounting wasn't it?'

'Well, yes, that's right, but what it amounted to was a few mistakes on his travelling expenses and he'd put in for a slightly ambitious entertainment allowance for all the meetings he provides for. I'm sure there was no dishonest intention. A lot of the tea and biscuits he pays for himself.'

'If that's all it is then he should never have been suspended. I'll look into it myself. Thank you my boy. Leave it to me.'

Feeling much happier, Mervyn returned to the office to find Mr Openthwaite waiting for him.

'Where have you been, Davis?' he said, without preamble. 'There was nobody here to take calls and there was no note or anything. You can't just swan off as and when you please.'

'I'm sorry, Mr Openthwaite, but I had to see Councillor Matthews, and George is not available at present.' Mervyn didn't know how much Openthwaite knew about George's suspension. He hadn't been around for ages having 'swanned off' himself without telling anyone where he was going.

'And why did you go to see Councillor Matthews, I won't have you going over my head, do you hear?'

'Councillor Matthews asked me to go to see him – you weren't here.'

'Don't be impertinent. If I have business elsewhere it is no concern of yours. Now what was the meeting all about? You'd better come to my office and explain.'

It took a long time to explain what had been happening because Openthwaite kept interrupting, but eventually Mervyn had been able to bring his boss up to date with events.

'You are in charge here while I'm away, Davis, you should never have allowed George to be suspended. I can't do without him, as you know.'

'None of us can do without him, I'm sure, but I had no say in the matter. Councillor Matthews is going to see what he can do to get George reinstated.'

'Humph!' said Openthwaite. Mervyn took that to mean the interview was terminated and he left the room.

'Davis!' shouted Openthwaite as Mervyn was about to enter his own office. 'Get me a cup of tea, and a biscuit – chocolate!'

'Coming up,' shouted Mervyn, and then quieter, 'Your Lordship.' He went into the kitchen and put on the kettle. He looked in all the cupboards but could find no biscuits of any kind. 'He'll have to do without,' he muttered, 'He's got a bloody nerve complaining about me swanning off, when he's never here himself,' Mervyn checked himself in case he had been speaking out loud.

13

Councillor Matthews phoned early the following morning. 'Good news, young Davis,' he said, 'Tell George I'd like to see him, would you. This morning if he can manage it. I'll fill you in later. Bye for now.'

Intrigued, Mervyn phoned George at home and told him to get round to the Town Hall as soon as possible to see Councillor Matthews.

'Oh, thanks, Mervyn, do you think he's been able to get me off the hook?'

'I don't know, but it certainly sounds promising. Let me know how you get on.'

'Will do. See you later.'

By lunchtime, nothing had been heard from George or the councillor, and Mervyn was getting anxious. Perhaps the councillor had come up against opposition in his attempt to reinstate George.

It was mid afternoon, Mervyn was thinking about making a cup of tea, when he heard the front door bang and footsteps clattering up the wooden stairs. It was George, his face split by a huge grin.

'You'll never guess, Mervyn, never in a million years. I can't believe it myself.'

'Come on, George, tell me, what has happened?'

'I'll have to show you, come downstairs.'

George led the way downstairs and into the car park. Two identical Volkswagen cars stood side by side. One of them was Mervyn's.

'They've given me a car! Can you believe it? My own car, just like yours. Isn't it great?'

'It is, George, it's wonderful. Tell me more. What did Matthews say?'

'Well, I'll need a cup of tea and a biscuit before I can tell you. I'm so excited. Come on.' He led the way back up to the office and Mervyn went to the kitchen to put on the kettle.

'We've no crackers, George, shall I go across to Singh's?'

'No, never mind, I'll manage without the crackers this time.' He took a deep breath, 'I've been promoted! I'm to be known as Senior Co-ordinating Officer. There isn't a junior co-ordinating officer yet, but just in case they want to appoint someone, I am assured of the senior position. Councillor Matthews did it. He told the Human Resources people that I was indispensable and as such I needed to be given a senior position and a senior salary to go with it. Isn't it wonderful?'

'That is wonderful news, George, I am so happy for you. So what does it involve, this new position?'

'Oh, I just carry on doing what I've always done, don't worry. I'll still be working here. It's just that now I am recognised. Nobody realised what I did until I wasn't here, did they?'

'That's very true, George, I thought the whole division would come tumbling down round my ears. I was getting ready to resign because I thought if I didn't I would get the sack.'

'Is his nibs in?' asked George, when he had finished his first cup of tea.

'No, he came in yesterday and threw his weight about, but he's gone off again.'

'I can't wait to tell him,' said George, 'What do you think he'll say?'

'I dread to think. I think it highly likely he'll have heart attack.'

George giggled.

14

George reminded Mervyn that it was his turn to provide the cracker biscuits so he walked across the road to Singh's Emporium to get some. He thought he would buy some nicer biscuits as well. They deserved them after all.

Mr Singh himself was serving and he greeted Mervyn with his usual courtesy.

'Good Morning, Sir, thank you for your custom. Is there anything else I can get for you today? We have some special offers . . .'

'No, I think those will do, thanks very much,' said Mervyn and he was about to leave the shop when Mr Singh called him back.

'Oh, excuse me, Sir. I'm thinking you are working at the council . . .'

'Yes, that's right, I work over the road at Hardcastle House. Can I help you with something?

'I think maybe you can. Do you know the game of volleyball?'

'I know of it of course, but I don't play it, in fact I don't think I have ever seen it played.'

'It is very popular game in Punjab where I come from, and we have here in Hindthorpe many Indian mens like me who are playing volleyball. It is one of the world's most popular games you know. It is, it is, I assure you. What I am wanting to ask is this. Can we use the tennis courts for a volleyball tournament?

'I really don't see why not, I'll find out for you. Would it involve altering the court in any way?'

'The lines would have to be marked differently and of course we have a different net. It is much higher than tennis. But we would be putting it all back together again afterwards. I want to invite teams from all over the country to take part. It would be good for Hindthorpe.'

Yes, I suppose it probably would. How long would you need the courts for?'

'Two weeks.'

'Mm. It's an interesting idea. Leave it with me, Mr Singh, and I'll get back to you.'

'My name is Gian, Mr . . .'

'Oh, sorry, Mervyn, Mervyn Davis,' Mervyn offered his hand and Mr Singh shook it enthusiastically.

'Thank you so much, Mr Mervyn, thank you.'

When Mervyn returned to the office, he told George about his conversation with Mr Singh.

'I don't know about that, Mervyn. They're tennis courts, not volleyball. You'd have to ask at the sports hall, I expect. We take bookings for the courts as you know, but it's their baby really. They do all the maintenance and stuff.'

'Who should I talk to up there?'

'Paul Sparrow is in charge up there. I don't have anything to do with that side of things.'

'Is his number in the book?'

'I shouldn't think so, I've never rung him.'

'Perhaps I'll just call in, casual like, and then bring it up in conversation. What do you think?'

'Could do. Wouldn't hurt. When are you going?'

'Well, now perhaps.'

'What, before you've had your coffee?'

'Well, no, not before I've had my coffee,' he laughed. 'Have you got it on?'

'Of course, it'll be ready in a minute.'

Mervyn knew where the sports hall was, but he, like George, had had no occasion to go there before. It was an impressive new building, set in extensive grounds. Mervyn could see goal posts for both association football and rugby as he drove round to the car park which was well filled with cars, even at this early hour.

Mervyn asked for Paul Sparrow at reception, explaining who he was and that it was just a social call.

'I'll see if I can find him. He'll be on one of the courts I daresay,' said the receptionist. She picked up a microphone and said 'Mr Sparrow to reception, please. Mr Sparrow. Gentleman to see you.' The Tannoy came through very loudly and Mervyn felt sure that wherever Mr Sparrow was he would hear.

After exchanging pleasantries, Mr Sparrow offered to show Mervyn round his facility. Mervyn was very impressed. He had no idea the borough's sporting residents were so well provided for.

'This is wonderful, Mr Sparrow, I'm very impressed,' said Mervyn, wondering how best to broach the subject of the volleyball tournament.

'Do you have facilities for volleyball here?'

Oh yes, the Indians play a lot. It's a very popular sport on the sub-continent.'

'So I understand. How would you feel about having a volleyball tournament on the tennis courts in Memorial Park Road?'

'They are tennis courts, Mervyn, specifically for tennis. That's why they are called tennis courts,' he smiled.

'Yes, I know, obviously, but if they were to be used for volleyball for a couple of weeks surely that wouldn't be too terrible would it?'

'But what about the people who want to play tennis?'

'They would only have to give up a couple of weeks.'

'But why should they?'

'Because a volleyball tournament would be a very good event to put on and would be very popular. It would also attract people from all over the UK to Hindthorpe.' Mervyn was warming to his argument.

'No, I don't think that would be possible. As I said, they are specifically tennis courts and they are in constant use as such.'

'I don't think that is quite true, is it? We deal with bookings for the courts at Hardcastle House and there really aren't that many requests.'

'I'm not prepared to argue with you, Mr Davis. I'm sorry. I can't allow the courts to be used for anything other than their original purpose. I'm sorry if that is what you came here to ask. Now, I'm very busy, so if you don't mind.'

Very well, I'm sorry you are taking that attitude. I shall have to go and explain to our Indian friends that you won't help them. Goodbye.'

Mervyn was very disappointed to be turned down. He had felt sure the idea would be well received. Openthwaite was off again on one of his lecture tours, so Mervyn couldn't ask his advice, so he decide to talk to his friend, Councillor Matthews about it.

Back at Hardcastle House, Mervyn told George what had happened at the sports hall.

'I told you, didn't I?' said George.' What are you going to do now? Talk to Matthews?'

'Yes, how did you guess?'

'That's what you always do, that's why,' laughed George.

Councillor Matthews was very interested in the idea for a volleyball tournament and promised to talk to some of the other councillors about it. They might even sponsor it and provide a cup for the winner, he thought.

Mervyn was delighted. He felt the chances of the tournament going ahead were so much better, it was worth reporting back to Mr Singh.

The other councillors were as enthusiastic as Matthews, and it was put to the vote in the full council meeting. The mayor himself offered to provide a cup, and by the end of the meeting they were talking about an annual tournament that would attract players, not only from the

UK, but from all around the world. It would be a wonderful thing for Hindthorpe to be a venue for an international sporting event. Whose idea was this, they wanted to know.

The tournament was scheduled for the end of August after most of the other regular events in the borough. Paul Sparrow, forced to accept the ruling of the council, had adopted the tournament wholeheartedly and allowed people to think it had been his idea all along.

Publicity had been handled by the press office and posters appeared on every hoarding in the town and advertisements were placed in all the national newspapers and the sporting press. Enquiries from countries all over Asia flooded in and Mervyn and George were overwhelmed by phone calls.

The tennis courts were cleaned and repaired where necessary and courts were marked up for volleyball. Local teams could be seen playing every night of the week, and because there were so many requests it was decided to install floodlighting so that the opening times could be extended. There was not one complaint from the tennis players that their courts had been taken over.

The Volleyball Tournament turned out to be one of the most successful events of the year. Hundreds of people from all over the world descended on Hindthorpe and all the hotels and guesthouses were full. The field behind Hardcastle House became a campsite with hundreds of tents housing the teams. A large mobile catering trailer was set up in the grounds to feed the players. It was all tremendously exciting.

On the last day the Mayor presented to cup to the winning team, not, unfortunately, one of the local teams, but one from Russia, another country where volleyball is evidently more popular than football. The winning team promised to come back next year, as did most of the other participants.

Mervyn was hailed as hero of the day by Mr Singh, whose grin had become a permanent fixture on his face from the outset.

'You should be Sikh, Mr Mervyn, you should, you should!' he said excitedly.

'Thank you Gian, I am honoured that you should think so. I am so pleased it has all worked out so well.'

Even Cyril Openthwaite, who had only returned from one of his lecture tours when the arrangements were too well established for him to interfere and disrupt, had been gracious enough to say 'Well done' to Mervyn.

15

At last the show season was over and Mervyn felt he could allow himself a holiday. Happy to leave George in charge, he confidently approached his boss for permission to take a fortnight's leave.

'Well, if you think the department can manage without you for a fortnight, I wonder what you do all day when you are here,' was the predictable response from Mr Openthwaite. Mervyn thought he must have a poor opinion of his own worth if he applied the same criterion to himself.

'At this time of year, things quieten down a little. I wouldn't have asked to take leave in the summer obviously. George is perfectly able to cope on his own.'

'Very well, but leave a contact address, just in case we need to get in touch.'

'Fat chance,' thought Mervyn, but said, 'Of course, I'll leave it with George.'

Mervyn had been looking forward to a holiday in his beloved France and now he was going. Two whole weeks without Openthwaite and councillors and meetings and leaky swimming pools. Bliss.

Mervyn had been going to his favourite place in France for many years, and, although he knew it almost as well as he did his home town, he felt no inclination to explore new places. The tiny gite where he always stayed was convenient, comfortable and reasonably priced. The people in the farm nearby were friendly and pretended that Mervyn's French was excellent, despite the fact that they sometimes didn't know what he was trying to say. A Gallic shrug and a laugh was often all the reply needed anyway. Mervyn had e-mailed Mme Grospote the day after the last show to confirm that the gite was free. He was disappointed to learn that the agreement for the use of his car did not include travel abroad so he was very glad he had kept the old SAAB. The ferry was booked, his bags packed and he was off.

While enjoying a glass of red wine, sitting outside his favourite café, a few days into his holiday, Mervyn smiled at the thought of the pompous Openthwaite, faced with some situation for which he could blame his liaison officer. George would pretend to know nothing and Openthwaite would have to deal with it himself. But Mervyn knew that would not happen, someone would be found to blame. Openthwaite had not felt the need to contact Mervyn, which was just as well as he hadn't left a forwarding address with George.

'*Encore du vin, Monsieur?*' asked the pretty waitress, breaking his reverie.

'*Oui, merci, c'est tres bien,*' said Mervyn, holding up his empty glass.

'*Vous voudrais manger Monsieur?*' she asked.

'*Oh, oui, merci.*'

The waitress produced a menu and Mervyn scanned the dishes on offer. He was not an adventurous eater and many of the dishes were as yet untried. He would have liked to try something different but his French was not good enough to be able to ask what the food was, and he was wary of ordering something which he might not like. He settled for a simple fish dish. The waitress smiled and whisked away the menu.

The food was delicious, and if it was the same as he'd had the day before it didn't matter. It didn't matter at all.

After his lunch, Mervyn took a stroll along the harbour and admired the many boats moored there. He spotted a tattered red ensign, hanging limply from the stern of a handsome yacht, and he waved to the owner as he passed.

Days passed lazily, Mervyn soaked up the atmosphere and the sun in equal measure and each evening when he returned to the tiny apartment, he felt pleasantly tired and thoroughly relaxed. This was the life, he thought. The only thing missing was someone to share it with. His rather peripatetic lifestyle before getting the job at the council had precluded forming lasting relationships and he had always been happy with his own company, but now he was conscious of a need for companionship, perhaps even love . . .

When the holiday eventually came to an end and Mervyn bade the Grospotes and their many animals *au revoir*, he felt a sense of loss. It was more than the sadness he always felt when leaving France, it was something he could not put his finger on.

16

'Morning George!' called Mervyn as he was about to enter the office and heard familiar clattering from the kitchen at the end of the corridor.

'Oh, Mervyn, you're back!' exclaimed George with evident delight. 'How was it, you didn't send me a postcard!'

'Oh, I did George, I expect it will arrive one day in the week. I don't know what they do with the post in France, probably send it by donkey cart I expect.'

'So, tell me, what was it like? Did you have good weather? And the food, what was the food like. Oh, I'd love to go to France.'

'I'll tell you about it over coffee, George, later. But first, what have we on the agenda?'

'Oh, well, this morning we have a meeting with the further education advisor, he wants to set up some classes for unemployed Asian ladies and he thought we could have them here.'

'Here, George? But we haven't any suitable rooms to hold classes in.'

'Well, no, not at present we don't, but they want to build an extension at the back . . .' George saw Mervyn's expression and stopped. 'I know, but don't ask me, I only work here. It was all the idea of your friend and mine, Mr Cyril Openthwaite, MBE.'

'What? MBE? I didn't know he had an MBE, how did that happen?'

'You wouldn't believe it would you, not if you didn't work for Hindthorpe Borough Council. Yes, the notification came through last week. His Nibs was chuffed to bits of course. He got it for services to the community or something.'

'So, he hasn't actually been to the palace yet then?'

'No, but he's telling everybody he's an MBE. He now thinks he is some sort of super being and he's got all these grand ideas. I think he's angling for a knighthood.'

'Heaven help us, George. So, they are going to build an extension and hold adult education classes here at Hardcastle House? I've never heard anything so daft. Why can't they use a community centre, or a school?'

'They, that is, His Nibs, says there are aren't any suitable venues where the Asian ladies can have privacy.'

'Why do they want privacy? If the classes are designed to help them into work they won't have privacy will they?'

'No, well, you know and I know, that the real reason for the classes is to butter up the Asian community. That's my guess anyway.'

'You'd better not be heard to say that, George.'

'I didn't say anything,' said George, miming a zipped lip.

'OK, so this guy is coming this morning is he? Is Himself meeting him, or us?'

'Himself, as you so aptly call him, is not here, we will greet the man and give him a tour of the facilities.'

'That shouldn't take long,' laughed Mervyn.

'No, so I thought we could give him coffee and biscuits first. What do you think?'

'Better get some decent biscuits then. I'll pop over to Singh's, do we need anything else over there?'

'Coffee, sugar, milk, er, biscuits of course, and a copy of the Daily Mail.'

'What's the Daily Mail for, a tablecloth?'

'No, silly, the cross-word.'

The Further Education Advisor, a tall but stooped man with grey hair and beard, was pleased with his tour of the premises and with his coffee and biscuits. He said he looked forward to the extension being built and subsequently working with Mervyn and George when the classes got under way. He had lots of ideas for classes and felt sure they would be well received. Mervyn and George were less pleased at the prospect, not least because it would mean Hardcastle House was no longer their exclusive domain.

Mervyn and George sat quietly dispatching the remainder of the fancy biscuits Mervyn had bought for their guest, when the phone shook them from their thoughts.

'Hello, Liaison . . . Yes, that's right, yes, oh, I see. Oh, thank you, that's very kind. What time? Three o'clock? Yes, we'd love to come, thank you. Bye.'

'What was that. Mervyn?' asked George, who had heard 'yes, we'd love to come','

'*Apna hi gar samajihi,*' said Mervyn.

'What?'

'*Apna hi gar sama jihi,* I think,' said Mervyn.

'I thought that was what you said. What does it mean?'

'I've absolutely no idea, but whatever it is we are invited. This afternoon at three o'clock at the Riverside Centre.'

'Well, who was it on the phone?'

'I don't know, an Indian lady I think, she sounded Indian. We'll have to go, George, I said we would.'

'Oh, that's OK, I don't mind going. I would like to know what we going to, though. I've never heard of that particular group.'

Apna hi gar sama jihi, or something that sounded very much like that, was an Indian ladies social group that met at the Riverside Community Centre every Monday afternoon. They did various crafts and exchanged gossip and generally had a jolly time, the genial lady in the colourful sari explained, when Mervyn and George arrived at the centre. Today, they deduced, was a festival day for one of their gods and an excuse for a feast. Tables were laid with dozens and dozens of little dishes of colourful food, none of which looked to Mervyn and George anything like the offerings of the average Indian restaurant. They were encouraged to tuck in by the ladies, all of whom were dressed in very beautiful saris and bedecked with gold jewellery.

'Ve vanting to share our food and our culture, you know. It is, it is. Yes, yes, eat, eat,' said the lady who seemed to be in charge of the food.

George and Mervyn tucked in. The food was delicious, some was hot and spicy some was sweet and rather sticky, but it was all wonderful. They ate with their fingers as did the ladies. Cups of tea were handed round and the ladies giggled delightedly when George and Mervyn expressed their appreciation of the food.

'Try this,' urged a tiny elderly lady in a vivid green sari.' She wrapped a red vegetable in a piece of soft flat bread and spread a dollop of chutney on it before handing it to Mervyn. 'Eat, enjoy,' she said.

Mervyn bit into the morsel and began to chew. He felt as if his mouth was full of wasps as the hot chilli took effect. 'Water!' he gasped, and tried to remove the food from his burning mouth onto a napkin. 'My God! What was that? My mouth is on fire,' he spluttered. The ladies were in hysterics. They thought it was hilarious. But then, when they saw that Mervyn was really in distress, they apologised and offered him soothing spoonfuls of yoghurt to ease the pain.

'So sorry, Mr Mervyn, we did not realise that you would not be able to take the heat. That is special delicacy, treat for honoured guest.'

'Well, thank you. I am pleased to be an honoured guest, but that was too much for me, I'm afraid.'

The ladies made a fuss of Mervyn and bade him sit to watch a display of traditional dancing. Frequent cups of tea helped to calm down his burning mouth.

After about an hour, during which George and Mervyn had been royally entertained,

113

they made their excuses, thanking the ladies for their hospitality and their friendship.

'You did well to avoid that particular delicacy George,' said Mervyn when they were sitting in the car. I've never had such pain. I thought I would die!'

'Well, I was not the honoured guest evidently,' said George, laughing. 'But the rest of the food was fantastic wasn't it?'

'It was indeed. And what a nice bunch of women.'

'Did you find out what apna gee thingy meant?'

'No, I forgot to ask.'

17

Much to Mervyn's surprise and delight, a set of plans for the proposed conversion of the sports pavilion into a youth centre, arrived on his desk by courier from the architects' department.

'Look at this, George!' Mervyn exclaimed, when he had scanned through the large sheets of drawings. 'Plans for my youth centre!' He beckoned George over to see.

'Gosh, Mervyn, that's amazing. You must have made a good impression on the architects. They don't usually act so quickly.'

'No, I think it is only that nice Robin Stroud that showed me the buildings that might be converted. He doesn't seem like the rest of them.'

'And these are from him, are they?'

'Yes, he's taken it on himself to produce some plans – just ideas really, at this stage, but they look promising. Whether I can get approval for the conversion is another thing entirely, I fear. I'll talk to Openthwaite and then, if he agrees, I'll put it to Matthews. If he likes the idea it could go to the council. What do reckon, George – a year?'

'Huh! You may be right. Still it's worth trying. Best of luck.'

And so Mervyn waited patiently for Openthwaite to come in to the office and when he did, a week later, he tentatively presented him with a written outline of his proposal and the plans. Openthwaite was suspicious and sceptical as usual, and reluctant to admit that the idea was sound, but he relented and gave Mervyn the go-ahead to talk to Councillor Matthews. Mervyn wasted no time, he phoned the councillor and made an appointment to see him that very afternoon.

Councillor Matthews was delighted with Mervyn's proposal and the professional way he had presented it. 'I think I can put this before the council as it is, Mervyn, my boy,' he said. 'It is about time we provided some facilities for the young people of the borough. This could be the start of something big.'

Mervyn's eyebrows almost met his hairline. 'Really, do you think so?'

'I do, I really do. Well done, my boy! I'm proud of you.'

Predictably, it was quite a while before the councillor was able to present Mervyn's proposals but when he did the response was positive. Detailed plans would be drawn up and the whole project would be costed. A planning application was submitted, based on the original plans. Everyone would hold their breath.

Less than six weeks after Mervyn's proposal had been presented to the council, he received a phone call from Councillor Matthews.

'Hello, Davis, Matthews here. Good news, my boy. It's been approved. Work can start almost immediately. I'd like to buy you a drink to celebrate. How about this evening. Meet me at the Royal Arms Hotel, say half past seven, what do you say?'

'That is absolutely wonderful, Councillor. Thank you. I would love to have a drink with you.'

The Royal Arms Hotel is the best hotel in the town and the haunt of all the top businessmen as well as many of the councillors, so Mervyn had to dress appropriately. His suit had not seen the light of day since his interview and it needed a brush up. He put on a new tie and polished his only pair of shoes. He was excited.

'The councillor was waiting for him in the lounge and with him was another man that Mervyn didn't recognise.

'Mervyn, my boy, good to see you. This is Andrew Gooding, he's the county youth officer. I told him about your project and he was keen to meet you, so I brought him along. I hope you don't mind.'

'I'm delighted to meet you, Mr Gooding, thank you for taking an interest in my idea.'

'Call me Andrew, Mervyn, and it is my pleasure, I assure you. We don't get many suggestions like yours and I am sure the service will benefit form this sort of innovation. There must be lots of redundant buildings that could be put to good use like this and there are precious few youth centres in the county. It might be just what is needed to get the ball rolling.'

Drinks were ordered and the three men settled down to discuss finer points of Mervyn's idea. Gooding wanted to know if Mervyn had any experience in youth work and what it was that inspired him to want to make provision for the young people of the borough.

'I met some of the local lads where I live and they told me they had nowhere to meet and that the community centres didn't let them in, so I thought I would see what could be done. I have no experience in youth work whatsoever, I'm afraid.'

'Well, there are many who would claim to have experience who haven't made such a valuable contribution to youth work, that's for sure.'

The evening passed pleasantly, Mervyn felt completely at ease with his important companions and they treated him as an equal. When he finally bade them goodnight he was glowing.

18

As part of the plan to hold further education classes at Hardcastle House an extension was to be built and groups of men could be seen standing around looking at the existing buildings, and men with theodolites did whatever it is that men with theodolites do.

George and Mervyn watched anxiously from their office window as the men came and went over a period of several weeks.

Cyril Openthwaite for once was much in evidence. He could be seen almost daily, conversing with the surveyors and architects.

He reported to Mervyn that the plans had been drawn up and that the extension would be built on the south side of the building, next to the children's playground. It also happened to be almost next to Mervyn's office and would block part of his view. He would no longer be able to see the tower blocks or the bend in the river and the few bits of greenery that survived the borough's urban sprawl.

'I think it is a pity they have decided to build on that side, further away from the entrance to the building,' Mervyn said.

'The further education department will have its own entrance of course,' said Openthwaite.

'I see. What will my involvement be exactly?'

'Yours?' said Openthwaite, 'You are responsible for it, I told you that.'

'But I have had no involvement in the discussions and I have not been consulted at all.'

'Why should you have been. I am in charge here, I make the decisions.'

'But surely, if I am to be responsible for running the centre, shouldn't I have some say in its establishment?'

'Not at all. That is my area of management. I set it up, as, I should remind you, I set up Hardcastle House in the first place. You, as Liaison Officer will see to its everyday running. It seems simple enough to me.'

I'm sorry to disagree with you, Mr Openthwaite, but I should remind you, that my expertise does not extend to further education, and if I am to be responsible for the running of an adult education centre I should at least have some training.'

'I can't see what training you need. All you have to do is set up classes, recruit teachers

121

and trainers, provide the necessary facilities, advertise the classes and receive payments from participants. Anybody could do that. Now, I'm busy, so, if you've no more to say.' He stood up and made it clear that Mervyn should leave his office.

'Well, I'm damned, George,' Mervyn said when he returned to his own office, 'I don't believe that man.'

'Cup of coffee?' suggested George, quietly.

'Thanks George, and a biscuit. Have we any of those posh ones left?'

Part of the plan to build an adult education centre involved removing the old tennis court at the rear of Hardcastle House. It had been disused for years but there had always been the hope that one day something would be done with it. Now Mervyn had an idea.

'George,' he said, 'that tennis court out the back.'

'Yes.'

'How big is it?'

'Roughly the size of a tennis court I would say as a guess,' said George.

'Right, but how big is that?'

'Why, what are you thinking, I can see twinkle in your eye, you're up to something.'

'You're right. I'm thinking go-kart track. What do you say?'

'Go-kart track, what, on the tennis court?'

'Yes, why not, I reckon it would be big enough. The tarmac is already there and it has a fence all round it. It would just need some old tyres to mark out a track and Bob's your uncle.'

'And some very expensive go-karts, and somewhere to keep them. And someone to run it. I think this might be an idea too far, Mervyn.'

'No, don't you see, if we are to have adult education, we could also have youth facilities. I have contacts in the youth service now. I could get things moving.'

George was not sure about Mervyn's idea but said no more. He had other things to worry about.

Mervyn couldn't wait to test his idea on someone who might receive it with more enthusiasm that had George. He phoned Andrew Gooding at County Hall, said he had an idea he would like to talk over, and could he come to County Hall to discuss it?' Andrew Gooding said of course, and they arranged to meet the next day.

Andrew Gooding thought it was an absolutely wonderful idea, and promised to investigate. There was nothing like it in the county and it would be a tremendous boost to his department if they were able to set it up. He was very grateful. Mervyn left County Hall feeling he was walking on air. He decided not to mention his idea to Openthwaite just yet.

He did tell George of his meeting with the youth officer and George warned him of the consequences of upsetting Cyril Openthwaite.

'If he thinks you are trying to thwart his plans he'll find a way of getting rid of you, Mervyn, I warn you. He's done it before. He's dangerous.'

'I know, George, but it's worth the risk. I am determined to get a fair deal for the young people of this town and if it means treading on His Nibs' toes, then so be it. Don't worry, I have big guns on my side.'

As good as his word, Andrew Gooding, the youth officer, had investigated the feasibility of installing a go-kart track on a tennis court. He had spoken to members of a go-karting club and they thought a track on a tennis court would be a bit tight but not impossible. Several of the karters had offered to come and have a look. They would be arriving at Hardcastle House on Wednesday morning. Things were moving fast.

Fortunately, Cyril Openthwaite, MBE, was not in on Wednesday. The karters arrived in a large truck, from which they unloaded two go-karts, several crash helmets, racing overalls and cans of fuel.

They introduced themselves to Mervyn and George and asked to see the tennis court.

'We thought we might as well try running the karts round to get a feel of the size of the track,' they explained. 'Have you ever tried karting?'

Mervyn said he hadn't, but would love to have a go. They wheeled the carts over to the tennis court and after a lot of preparation and explaining to Mervyn how to drive the vehicles they tried a few circuits.

'Wow! That's terrific fun,' said Mervyn after whizzing round at what seemed like breakneck speed. 'This will be great for the local youth.'

George, who had been watching from the office window, intending to keep out of it, could resist no longer and came down to join in the fun.

'Can I have a go?' he said, looking longingly at the tiny vehicles speeding round and round the tennis court.

'Of course, find yourself a helmet and there are some overalls there too,' offered one of the karters.

Soon, Mervyn and George were chasing round the track after each other, their faces split with huge grins.

'You need to get a load of old tyres, most garages will let you have some because they normally have to pay to have them removed.

Then we can make a proper track layout. You'll be surprised what an interesting circuit we can create.' Tony, the owner of the kart club explained.

When they were able to tear themselves away from the karts they all went upstairs to Mervyn's office where George provided coffee and biscuits. He had been over to Singh's for extra supplies.

'I hope this has been useful,' began Tony, we've had fun and I know you have. I guess you just have to sell the idea to the people who make the decisions.'

'That's going to be the hard part, I fear, but I am going to try very hard. We are most grateful to you and your chaps for giving up your time to come over. It really has been wonderful.'

'We were more than happy, Mervyn, and if there's anything more we can do, just ask. When it comes to buying equipment, do get in touch because we can advise you where to shop.'

George, ever resourceful, had thought to take photographs of the karts and he presented Mervyn with a set of prints the following morning. 'I thought these might be useful when you are preparing your report on the karting idea.'

'George, you are marvellous. Why didn't I think of that. Thank you. These could make all the difference. I'm going to see Matthews later today so I'll prepare a nice dossier.

Councillor Matthews was shocked by Mervyn's suggestion of using the tennis court as a karting track, but after he had studied Mervyn's report and looked at the photographs, he was warming to the idea.

'Have you discussed this with your line manager, Mervyn?' he said, eventually.

'No, I haven't. Mr Openthwaite has not been in the office this week and I wanted to get the ball rolling. That's why I have approached you. I spoke to the county youth officer about it and he was delighted, in fact it was him that organised the visit from the karting club.'

'I fear Mr Openthwaite will not be pleased, Mervyn. I think you may have gone too far this time. I may not be able to help you.'

'I felt sure you would support me on this,' said Mervyn, now quite worried.

'Well, I do, in principle, but you know how difficult your boss is, and he does have influence. Hasn't he got some scheme going to put adult classes on at Hardcastle House?'

'Yes, he has and he wanted to remove the tennis court. That was what gave me the idea for a kart track, because I don't think we are in a position to offer adult education. None of us is qualified.'

'Yes, well, you may be right, but you can't just steamroller over a superior's ideas because you don't agree with them. It doesn't work like that. Oh dear, Mervyn, my boy, I think you are in deep trouble. Or you will be if you try to go ahead with this.'

'I think I am right, Councillor. And I mean to continue. This borough has gone on long enough without provision for young people and I have already started by getting approval for the conversion of the sports pavilion into a youth centre, and the kart track is the next step. I mean to find more buildings that can be converted, too.'

19

Cyril Openthwaite, MBE, returned from wherever he had been before Mervyn was able to gather his supporters for the go-kart project, and somehow the formidable Member of the British Empire had found out what was afoot.

'In my office, Davis, now!' he shouted as he came up the stairs. 'Conway! Coffee! And biscuits, for one!'

'Very good, Mr Openthwaite,' replied George, and under his breath he added, 'MBE.'

Mervyn stood in front of Openthwaite's desk. There was no chair, and in any case he would not have been invited to sit. This was not going to take long.

'Your behaviour has not been up to standard since you came on my staff, Davis, and now you have tried to destroy my plans. I demand loyalty from my staff, do you hear. This is nothing short of treason. Treason! I will not tolerate it. You can forget your youth clubs and your go-kart tracks. Go-karts! I've never heard such nonsense. Do you hear? You are, from this minute, suspended from duty. There will be an inquiry, and if I have anything to do with it, you will be dismissed. Now go!'

Mervyn opened his mouth to speak, but seeing the expression on Openthwaite's face, he changed his mind and left the office quietly. He looked in to the kitchen where George was preparing coffee.

'He's suspended me, George. I'd better go. I hope I shall see you around. I don't know what will happen.'

'I am so sorry, Mervyn, but I did warn you. Best of luck mate. I will see you. Come down the Anvil and Hammer one night. Ok?'

'OK, George, Bye.'

Stopping only to pick up his coat from behind the office door, Mervyn left Hardcastle House and sat in his car. 'Now what do I do?' he asked himself.

A little later as he was getting out of his car in the car park next to Wilson Tower he heard his name called. He looked round but could see nobody.

'Here!' came the voice again. He looked up and there, leaning out of a second floor window, was Vanessa, from the swimming pool. 'Hello, Mervyn,' she called, 'Come up! Number 26. Have a cuppa.'

'Oh, OK, thanks, I will.'

Mervyn was pleased to find someone he knew in his tower and wondered why Vanessa was not at work. He took the stairs to the second floor and easily found number 26 – the door was open.

'Come on in, shut the door behind you. Tea or coffee?' Vanessa was calling from the kitchen at the end of the corridor so Mervyn joined her.

'Hello, fancy you being in my tower!' he said.

'Yes, fancy. I saw your car pull up and I thought it might be you. You don't see many cars that colour.'

'Why are you at home, are you not well?' Mervyn asked.

'It's my day off. I have to work Saturdays so I get a day off in the week. I'd rather be at work really because I get bored on my own. All my mates are at work. But why aren't you at work, aren't you well yourself?'

'I, um, I've been suspended.'

'Suspended! What for? Sorry, I shouldn't ask. Yes I should – why?'

Mervyn laughed, 'It's OK to ask. I have upset Mr Openthwaite I'm afraid. I went over his head once too often.'

'From what I hear that isn't difficult, to upset him I mean. What did you do?'

Over coffee and biscuits, Mervyn explained everything, and Vanessa listened sympathetically.

'You poor thing, that's awful,' she said eventually, and patted Mervyn's arm. 'What will you do?'

'I really don't know. I will have to talk to the county youth officer and explain that the go-kart track will be very unlikely to go ahead, and I'll have to keep in touch with Councillor Matthews, because he has been very helpful all the time I've been with the council.'

'Can't he help you with this, then?'

'No, he more or less said I was on my own with this. He doesn't think he can help. I think I have probably lost my job. Pity, because I was beginning to really enjoy it.'

'Are you in the union?' asked Vanessa, suddenly.

'Um, yes, well I don't have anything to do with it, but I pay my subscription. Do you think they might be able to help?'

'That's what they are there for, surely. Do you know who your rep is?'

'No idea. As I say I've not had anything to do with the union at all.'

'I should think your rep will the same as mine – Sid Meadows from the Depot, the transport place you know, where you go with your expenses?'

'Oh, yes, of course. Yes, I think I know who Sid is. Do you think I should speak to him?'

'I would. It can't do any harm. Then you'll be represented when it comes to the inquiry.'

'Vanessa, you're a treasure, I would never have thought of that. Thank you very much. And thanks for coffee too. I feel much better now. I'd better get off and see Sid. Thanks again.'

Sid was very helpful and said he didn't think Mervyn would lose his job; not if he had anything to do with it. He wanted all the details of the disagreements Mervyn had had with Openthwaite since he started with the council and urged him to keep in touch and let him know the minute he had any correspondence about the case.

Rather than going to see Councillor Matthews – he wasn't sure if he was even allowed access to the Town Hall while he was suspended – Mervyn wrote him a letter with all the details of his dispute with Openthwaite.

There was nothing more he could do, so he sat in his flat and watched daytime television until he was bored.

He remembered George's invitation to see him at the Anvil and Hammer, and as he wasn't even sure if he was still allowed to use the Golf, went in the SAAB, grateful that he had kept it taxed and insured.

He was too early for the pub when he arrived at the canal-side so he walked along the towpath, watching the ducks and swans. It was a beautiful evening and had he not felt he had all the cares of the world on his shoulders he would have enjoyed his walk.

It began to get quite dark and if he was not careful he might miss his footing on the muddy towpath and fall in the canal. His body would be found and they would conclude that he had committed suicide. He smiled wryly. No, that would not do at all. That was not the way he dealt with problems. He was a fighter. Openthwaite would not have his way. He smiled again, and quickened his step on his way back towards the pub.

'Hello, Mervyn! Good to see you,' said George, when Mervyn stepped into the dim interior of the Anvil and Hammer. 'I didn't know if you would come. Meet the lads, this is Steve, he's an ace pool player, this is Gordon, captain of the darts team, and of course, you've already met Andy, the landlord.'

'Hi, guys, good to meet you. Er, can I get you all a drink?'

Mervyn enjoyed the company and found that he had a natural aptitude for pool, a game he had never played before. It was closing time before he knew where the time had gone and by that time he was feeling quite merry.

'You'd better come home with me I think, Mervyn, you're not fit to drive,' said George as he helped Mervyn to the door.

'I think you're right. It's along time since I had so much to drink.'

Mervyn was pleased to see Jackie again and was introduced to their daughter, Petal.

When Mervyn had been looking for George on the day of the show, he had found the house but had not been inside. Now he was surprised how well cared for it was. The outside was untidy and strewn with all manner of rubbish, suggesting that the house might be the same. George must have sensed Mervyn's reaction and explained.

'We've had a lot of burglaries on the estate and the houses that get done are the ones that are well looked after, with tidy gardens and flowers and such. The scruffy ones are left alone. I guess the villains reckon we don't have anything worth stealing!' He laughed. It works. We've not been done since I put those old motor bikes in the garden and stopped cutting the grass. Three times before that. I was always buying new tellies!'

George had persuaded Mervyn to stay the night so it was morning before Mervyn returned to his flat. On the doormat were several letters from colleagues who had heard of his suspension, offering sympathy and support. Mervyn was amazed. He almost cried to think that people were so concerned.

He almost missed a small envelope that had got stuck upright against the skirting. He was surprised to that it had no stamp or address, but just had his name neatly written. Inside was a card from Vanessa with a picture of a cat and an invitation to call. She had included her mobile number.

Mervyn sat at his kitchen table drinking coffee and thinking about Vanessa's message. Did she have some news for him or was it simply a friendly invitation. He was intrigued. He picked up phone and punched in the number.

'Hi, Vanessa? It's Mervyn. Thanks for the card. That was nice of you.'

'Do you want to come round for a bit of company?' Vanessa said.

'That would be nice. Are you working just now?'

'I'm just leaving. I'll be home in about half an hour. Why don't I cook us something?'

'Well, I must say that sounds very nice indeed. What time should I come down?'

'Well, as I say I'll be back in half an hour, come when you like.'

'Great! See you soon then.'

This is an unexpected bonus, thought Mervyn, I might be on to a good thing here. He thought if he had been at work he would have popped across to Singh's to buy a bottle of wine, but the nearest shops were fifteen minutes away and he didn't want to seem too keen, not just yet. See how things work out. He did, however, have a shower and a shave and put on a clean shirt.

It was barely an hour later when he rode the lift down to the second floor of Wilson Tower and knocked on Vanessa's door.

'Hello, come on in, do you want to chop up some veg? We'll have a stir fry if that's OK.'

'Sounds good to me. How are you Vanessa? How's work?'

'I'm great thanks, and work is great, too. I love it at the swimming pool. They're a great crowd. It's a laugh.'

'It does sound a nice place to work – as long as the pool doesn't leak!'

'Oh, yes, that was a nightmare, still Hardeep sorted it for us thanks to you and George. The gala went off OK in the end.'

Vanessa didn't stop talking all the time she was cooking, and managed to talk pretty much all the time she was eating, too. Mervyn was happy to listen and to watch her – she was a very attractive young woman. She had a healthy tan, or was it her natural skin colour, he couldn't be sure, and blond hair tied into a short bunch at the back.

'What?' she said, suddenly stopping what she had been saying.

'Mm?' murmured Mervyn.

'You were looking at me funny.'

'Oh, I'm sorry, what do you mean, funny?'

'You were looking kind of dreamy.'

'I think I was thinking how nice you are,' admitted Mervyn, feeling a little embarrassed.

Vanessa leaned across the table and kissed him on the cheek. 'You're nice, too.' She laughed.

The rest of the evening passed for Mervyn in a kind of warm fuzz. Afterwards he couldn't remember much except that it had been very pleasant.

20

Mervyn was unable to settle to anything. The union representative, Sid Meadows, had put all the details of Mervyn's dispute with Openthwaite to the branch secretary and the lawyers had been consulted. There was really nothing useful Mervyn could do, but he couldn't just wait and do nothing. He paced the sparsely furnished living room of his penthouse flat – he liked to think of it as a penthouse although the only thing it had in common with the accepted idea of a penthouse was its altitude. The view from the balcony on a clear day was breathtaking, but if Mervyn looked down it made him feel quite queasy. He stood leaning on the metal railing and thought about his situation. He had only taken this job because he couldn't really think what he wanted to do. He'd had so many jobs, some he'd liked and some he hadn't. Some he'd positively hated – like the one selling expensive luggage in Saudi Arabia. How on earth had he finished up there? All those poor crocodiles. That job had been quite instructive – he now knew for sure that he was not a salesman. Did he really care if he lost this job? He enjoyed the work, and the people, and it seemed worthwhile. He was actually helping people, and that made him feel good. But was it what he wanted to do for the next few years? Not really. But he didn't want to have to leave because of an idiot like Openthwaite. He would fight. He smiled at the thought of winning and getting compensation for unfair dismissal and being offered reinstatement, and then resigning. That would be good. But it wouldn't be fair on the people who had helped him win his case. He would have to stay on for a while at least. But he wouldn't be able to work with Openthwaite. Perhaps they would sack him instead! He thought about Openthwaite, where did he go? George had told Mervyn that he gave lectures – where? And was he paid for them? You bet he was. And yet that was not allowed. The council forbade outside work. If you did voluntary work that was OK but even that had to be approved. Could he find out what he was up to and turn the tables on him? That was not in Mervyn's nature, but even so, Openthwaite had treated him badly from the start. It would serve him right.

Mervyn's mobile rang and shook him out of his reverie.

'Hello?'

'Hello, Mervyn, it's George. How's it going?'

'I'm OK, yes, OK, thanks, George. How are you?'

'OK, but I miss you, Mervyn. I have got used to our chats and our coffee breaks. It isn't the same in Hardcastle without you.'

'That's nice of you to say that, George . . .'

'But it's true. I tell you what, why don't we meet up for lunch one day?'

'OK, George, but remember I'm not supposed to talk to you.'

'We'll meet outside the borough then.'

They arranged to meet at a transport café on the bypass. George knew the man that ran it and he said the food was exceptional.

It was, if you liked three well fried eggs with about half a pound of bacon, tomatoes, mushrooms, onions and baked beans, followed up with sticky ginger pudding and custard and a pint mug of tea. George tucked into his plateful with gusto, while Mervyn, who was used to more modest portions, was less keen.

'What's the matter, Mervyn? Aren't you hungry?'

'I'm sorry, George, no, I don't seem to be.'

'I'll eat some of yours then, if you like, it's a shame to send it back, and I wouldn't want to hurt the chef's feelings.' He took Mervyn's plate and slid a good half of the food onto his own plate. 'There, you'll be able to eat that little bit.'

'I don't know what to do, George,' said Mervyn, when he had finished eating.

'What do you mean?'

'About the job. This suspension.'

'Didn't you say the union was dealing with it?'

'Yes, they are, but I don't know if they will be able to get me reinstated. I think old Openthwaite has quite a lot of clout in the department.'

'Yes, he does, but you'd be surprised how powerful the union can be. I wouldn't worry too much.'

'I was wondering if I could get back at Openthwaite in some way. George. He's been pretty mean to me ever since I started, and I've done nothing, until now that is, to deserve it. I'd just like to rock his boat a bit. Do you think there's any mileage in investigating his absences?'

'I think we've all wondered what he gets up to when he goes off. But I don't know how we'd find out what he's doing. All I do know is he gives a lot of lectures.'

'That's a starting point then. Where does he give the lectures?'

'I know he gave one recently at a university in the north of England somewhere. I got his train tickets for him. Where was it now? Oh, yes, of course, I remember. It was Brasford. I thought at the time, why would anybody want to go to Brasford University?'

'I've never heard of it, but is seems that every town has to have a university these days, now that practically all school leavers are expected to go to uni instead of being plumbers and brickies. No wonder there are so many Polish plumbers. It doesn't sound to me as if it would be a very big university does it, so it shouldn't be too difficult to find out what old Percy was lecturing about. Do you want to have a go at it, George?'

'Yes, I'll do that. I'll let you know how I get on.'

'There's not a lot more anybody can do really, George, so I think I'll just get back now and leave you to do a bit of sleuthing.

'That's OK, Mervyn, I'll be glad to do it. Don't worry.'

Mervyn got up, patted George's back affectionately, and left the café.

There was a letter on his doormat when he got back to the flat. 'Hand delivered, that's interesting,' he said to himself as he opened the envelope. 'Mm, from Sid Meadows, the union guy,' he muttered.

Dear Comrade,
I have been investigating the circumstances leading up to your suspension from your post as Liaison Officer and it appears that Cyril Openthwaite took it upon himself to suspend you. That being the case, your suspension is not official and theoretically you could resume your duties immediately. The only way anyone can be suspended is after an enquiry undertaken by the Human Resources Department and authorised by the Council. We, that is the branch, are looking into recommending disciplinary action against Percy Openthwaite. I hope this puts your mind at rest. I will let you know as soon as I hear anything further.

Regards,

Sid Meadows

'Brilliant!' exclaimed Mervyn, that's exactly what I needed. Old Perce won't know what hit him. I'd better tell George.' He realised he'd been talking to himself and laughed. 'I'm going barmy, but I don't care!' He laughed again. Calming down slightly, Mervyn sat down to think what he should do next. Not having a phone in the flat meant that he would have to go to see George and Councillor

Matthews to tell them what had transpired. Also Vanessa, who had suggested getting the union involved.

It soon became clear that Mervyn would not be able to continue working at Hardcastle House. The Chief Executive invited him to use an office in the Museum and suggested that perhaps it would make sense if he joined the Chief Executive's Department. It would be an appropriate move in the circumstances. This was a step up for Mervyn as the Chief Exec's department was the top drawer in the borough. He very quickly moved his few belongings from Hardcastle House into his new office, which, though very small, was luxurious compared to the one he shared with George. The office was equipped with a computer and a photocopying machine. There were two telephones on the desk, one of them a direct link to the chief himself. Mervyn was not conversant with computers but resolved to learn how to use it. The other staff, including the staff of the museum itself were very friendly and the curator offered to give Mervyn a guided tour of the exhibits. The only person who was not pleased with the new arrangement was George, who felt abandoned.

Apart from his change of address, Mervyn's work was much the same, and he quickly got down to business again following up requests for maintenance and advice from residents' associations and the various voluntary bodies that used the council's facilities.

The architects' department had done the necessary alterations to the disabled facilities at the community centre and Mervyn had a call from Phil Stevens of the West End Wheelers thanking him profusely.

'I don't know how you did it, Mr Davis, but they certainly moved quickly. Everything's hunky-dory now. The lads are delighted. Thank you very much indeed. Next time you are over this way, please call in to see us.'

'Well, I'm delighted too, of course, but I don't think it was all my doing. The Chief executive got onto it and he gets things moving pretty quickly.'

'But it was you that got him onto it wasn't it?'

'Well, yes I suppose it was.'

'There you are then. Don't put yourself down. We'll look forward to seeing you, Bye.'

Councillor Matthews was pleased to see Mervyn back again and was pleased to tell him that the council had approved the development of the old tennis courts into a go-kart track. They had set aside a sum of forty thousand pounds for the purchase of equipment and they were looking into appointing a part time instructor.

'That's fantastic, Councillor! Thank you very much.'

'Don't thank me, boy, it was all your doing. Well done. Oh, and that old sports pavilion you wanted to convert?'

'Yes,'

'They've approved that as well!'

'I don't believe it. That's fantastic.'

'Yes, and there's more. You remember Andrew Gooding, the County Youth Officer?'

'Of course, yes.'

'He wants another meeting. Do you want to give him a ring. I daresay it would be best if you went to see him at County Hall.'

21

Apart from the times when Mervyn joined George for coffee and cracker biscuits back at Hardcastle House when Openthwaite was out of the way, Mervyn had been taking his coffee breaks with the Museum Staff in their comfortable staff room. He became quite friendly with Stephanie, the receptionist, who had welcomed Mervyn so warmly on his very first visit to the Museum. They found they had many interests in common, and as the museum was not very busy during weekdays, except when there was a school visit, Stephanie would spend time in Mervyn's office, helping out on occasions with letters and phone calls.

One such occasion when Mervyn was struggling with the minutes of a meeting of primary school head-teachers that he had been invited to chair, Stephanie was phoning Hardeep to get him to repair some vandalised council houses on the West End estate.

'I had no idea, Mervyn, before you came to work here, just how much vandalism there is in the town. It's awful isn't it?'

I think it is probably no worse than in a lot of towns, but, yes, it is dreadful. I am not condoning it for a minute, but I am sure, if we were able to provide more facilities for young people, they wouldn't want to smash stuff up.'

'I'm sure you're right. I do think you are wonderful, trying to do all this for the youngsters.' She looked at Mervyn and beamed. 'You are quite a hero, you know.'

'Oh, nonsense,' said Mervyn, embarrassed.

'It's true. I heard from one of our neighbours. She has a teenage boy and he and his mates had been talking about you and his mother asked who they were talking about. They idolise you, those lads at the kart track. Did you know they call it the Mervyn Davis Kart Track?'

'You're having me on,' said Mervyn.

'No, I'm not, they say "Let's go down the Mervyn." They do!'

Mervyn didn't know what to say, so put his head down and continued typing.

'You're embarrassed aren't you, Mervyn? You should be pleased.'

'Of course I'm pleased it has all worked out. There was a time when it looked very unlikely to happen at all.'

'And it is all down to you,' said Stephanie. I think you are wonderful.'

Mervyn looked up at Stephanie. She was quite bonny, but not really overweight, she had short curly fair hair and freckles. She wore little if any make-up and it was difficult to estimate her age. Mervyn had not really taken proper notice of her, but now he saw a very attractive young woman who clearly liked him. He tried to concentrate on his minutes but found Stephanie very distracting.

'Do you like music, Mervyn?' asked Stephanie suddenly.

'Depends what sort of music, I like some, why?'

'Well, I thought being as you're from Wales, you probably would . . .'

'Just because I'm from Wales doesn't automatically make me like music you know,' answered Mervyn, perhaps a little sharply. It was something that was often said and it irritated sometimes.

'No, of course, but, well what kind of music do you like?' Stephanie persisted.

'I like a lot of classical, some jazz, not a lot of modern stuff or pop. Why?'

'It's just that it's the Concert in the Park on Saturday, here in the museum grounds. We do the refreshments and most of the staff come, even if they are not actually working. It's usually very good, we get musicians from all over. I wondered if you fancied coming.'

'I might do. Is there a programme?'

'I'll get you one, we've got them in reception.' She got up and left the room, leaving Mervyn wondering if she was inviting him to go with her or just mentioning it out of interest.

'There you are,' Stephanie said, thrusting a glossy programme in front of Mervyn and leaning close so she could point out items she thought would be of interest. Mervyn was almost overcome by her perfume at such close quarters and he felt slightly uncomfortable.

'They're playing a lot of ballet this time, I thought it looked good. What do you think?'

'Yes, I do like ballet. It's a long time since I saw one but, yes, it does look good. Perhaps I will come. Do I need a ticket?'

'We get concessions as staff, so you'll be all right. Or, if you fancied selling programmes or something, you could get in free.' She looked expectantly at Mervyn and he had to smile.

'No, I'd rather buy a ticket, I think. What are you doing?'

'I'm not working myself on Saturday. We could go together if you like.'

So she was inviting me to go with her, after all, thought Mervyn. Well, OK, why not. 'That would be very nice, Stephanie. Thank you. I'll look forward to it. Um, do people dress up. Ballet is usually quite a posh affair.'

'Not when it's outdoors, I don't think. No, just smart casual.'

The Concert in the Park was evidently one of the town's prestige events and so all the department heads and of course the mayor and his lady were there. Businessmen who wanted to make a good impression were there and the people who liked to be seen with the people who wanted to make a good impression were there, too. As were the press. Mervyn was amazed by the number of people at the event; a huge stage had been erected and seating for several hundred people was arranged in a large fan shaped block. The weather was fine and warm and most of the women wore summer dresses. Despite what Stephanie had said, people had dressed up for the event. Men wore either smart blazers and flannels or dinner jackets, Mervyn's old sports jacket seemed a little out of place but it didn't matter because it was getting dark already and the contrast between the bright lights on the stage and the dimmer light in the auditorium made him almost invisible.

Most of the seats were already occupied and there were as many people standing at the sides of the seating area. At first he couldn't see a single soul he recognised. Members of the orchestra were filing in and taking their seats, the buzz of conversation lessened and the people who always coughed at times like this, coughed. Then Mervyn spotted Stephanie, over the far side, in among a group of young people he didn't know. He made his way round the back of the seating and, just as the music started, he reached Stephanie's side. She appeared not to have seen him so he gently touched her arm.

'Hello, Mervyn, I thought you'd changed your mind. Sh, it's about to start,' she said, and turned away.

'The programme began with a medley of several short pieces from well known ballets, most of which were familiar to Mervyn. Then the conductor turned round and addressed the audience, explaining the programme and why he had chosen the music.

There was an air of great excitement in the park. Several hundred people were totally silent as they waited for the first piece to begin.

Mervyn turned to Stephanie and opened his mouth to speak, but she put her finger to her mouth and turned away, intent on the orchestra. Mervyn felt unwelcome. It was as if he hadn't been invited. Stephanie didn't acknowledge him at all throughout the first piece, the overture to Coppelia. He began to think he had misunderstood Stephanie. Surely it was more than just telling him about the concert – she had specifically invited him.

He wasn't enjoying the concert although the music was wonderful. In the first interval, Stephanie seemed to be relating to the people in her group, but not to him. He started to sidle away, nodding to people as he went, even though he didn't know them.

He felt hurt and rejected. He'd thought Stephanie was being more than just friendly, her approach had been what might be called a pass. But he was being silly, and felt even worse because he had made a fool of himself. He got into his car and waited for a loud passage of music before starting the engine and slowly leaving the car park.

At the museum on Monday morning, Mervyn avoided Stephanie and didn't go into the staff room for coffee. Instead he phoned George to ask if Openthwaite was in.

'Oh, Mervyn! I'm glad you called, no, His Nibs isn't in, come round for coffee. Bring some crackers with you, I've run out. See you in a bit.'

Mervyn parked in his usual place at the rear of Hardcastle House and ran up the stairs to George's office, which, he was interested to note, had been redecorated and supplied with new furniture. A smart new computer sat on George's desk.

'You've got a computer, George!'

'Yes, I don't know how to work it yet but they're going to send me on a course.'

'I've got one too, but all I've done with it so far is type up some minutes. I'm sure it will do all sorts of things when I get time to fathom it out. But, never mind about that. Why were you so keen for me to come round?'

'To see my new office. What do you think?'

'It's super, George. Things are looking up.'

'Yes, and what's even better – His Nibs isn't coming back.'

'What? What's happened? I haven't heard anything.'

'No, it isn't common knowledge, but after the business of your unauthorised suspension there was an investigation and they uncovered all manner of things that our Percy had been up to on the quiet. Apart from his lectures, he also had a job as a tutor in one of the red brick universities. Part time of course. That way he was able to put in an appearance here from time to time. He's got the sack. And, and you'll love this. He's got the sack from the uni as well!'

'I'm sorry to hear myself say this, George, but it serves him jolly well right for being so very unpleasant.'

'I knew you'd be pleased. And, there's more!' he chuckled – I am in charge of

Hardcastle House. Me, little old George, caretaker and dogsbody. Isn't it great?'

'I'm delighted for you, George. Do you get a nice big increase in salary?'

Well, as you know they already gave me a new job title and a rise, so I'm still on the same scale but at least I am on my way up.'

'So, what is it again – Chief Co-ordinating Officer?'

'Yes, that's the official title, but for everyday use I'm simply The Co-ordinator. I think that sounds even better don't you?'

'I do, George. Well done, you deserve it. Have you got the coffee on? I brought some crackers.'

22

Mervyn was due to see Andrew Gooding, the
County Youth Officer, at County Hall. He had
no idea what Gooding wanted to see him for.
He hoped it was not to tell him off for poking
his nose into youth service business.

'Ah, Mervyn, you don't mind me calling
you Mervyn? How nice to see you,' said
Andrew Gooding as he rose from his desk.
'Have a seat, can I get you coffee?'

'That would be nice, thank you,' said
Mervyn sitting.

The coffee arrived promptly, obviously
ordered before Mervyn arrived, in anticipation
of him saying he'd like a cup. Andrew fussed
with the cups for a minute and then came
round to Mervyn's side of the desk and sat
facing him. Mervyn liked that. Most people sat
behind their desks.

'I expect you're wondering why I asked to
see you, Mervyn,' Andrew began. You see, I've
had an awful job with Hindthorpe up to now,

as they've always resisted my attempts to get any appreciable youth provision into the borough. The government is talking about making it a statutory requirement, as I'm sure you know, to provide facilities for young people aged between thirteen and nineteen. Hindthorpe council have always maintained that their community centres more than satisfy the requirement, but of course, they don't . . .'

'The community centres won't allow the young people in unless they are signed up for some specific activity,' interrupted Mervyn.

'Exactly! And then you came along. We at County Hall are delighted with the projects you have initiated and we're keen to give you every assistance we can to get more provision in place.'

'That's good to know. I've had some difficulty up to now but I think one of the major obstacles has been removed – I'd rather not say any more, but let's just say things should be easier from now on.'

'I think I understand. Very well, we'll say no more about that.' Andrew made a noise between a laugh and a burp. He sat back and sipped his coffee, while studying Mervyn intently, as if he was trying to read his mind. Then, evidently having seen in Mervyn what he hoped to see, he leaned forward. 'Up to now we haven't had an area youth officer in the south of the county, and that may be part of the problem we've had trying to convince Hindthorpe to do more for youth, I don't know, anyway – now we have decided to appoint an area officer.'

'That would be good, I'm sure,' said Mervyn.

'Yes, and what would be even better would be if you were that area officer.' Andrew leaned back in his chair again.

'Me?' said Mervyn, taken aback.

'Yes, mind you, we would have to advertise the post and there would be interviews, but I'm sure, with your proven track record . . . '

'But I don't have a youth work qualification,' said Mervyn.

'I'm getting to that, bear with me. If you were to apply for this position and were successful, it would be necessary to obtain a qualification, but we could arrange for you to do a part-time post graduate diploma course. It can be done in a year, as in-service training. How does that sound?'

'You've taken me by surprise rather. I don't know.'

'Oh, I assume you do have a degree, Mervyn, it would be rather difficult to organise if you don't.'

'Oh, well yes, I do, not very relevant though. I read chemistry at Nottingham.'

That doesn't matter, as long as you have a degree, you can tack on further professional studies. So, what do you think?' he said impatiently.

'As I said, you have caught me unawares as it were. I had no idea this was on the cards. It sounds very appealing, I must say.'

'I knew you'd like it, so will you apply?'

'I'd like to give it some serious thought at my leisure, if you don't mind. It's a lot to take in.'

'I realise that, Mervyn. If you did go for it, and were successful of course,' he smiled, 'you would start in September. That would give you plenty of time to wrap up what you are doing in Hindthorpe, I imagine. You would have an office here in County Hall, but we would have to find a base somewhere in the south of the county as well. That can be sorted when the time comes.'

'Have you got a job description I can take home and study?' asked Mervyn, anxious not to be steam-rollered into something he might later regret.

'Of course, yes, sorry.' He leaned over his desk and picked up a folder which he handed to Mervyn. 'It's all here, full details of the job, the whole package, all about pensions and so on. Oh, and of course, I didn't mention the salary did I?' He mentioned a figure which Mervyn could not take in. While he was trying to make sense of the numbers, Andrew had stood and was holding out his hand.

'I'll look forward to hearing from you, Mervyn. I really do hope we can work together.'

Mervyn drove back to Hindthorpe in something of a daze. Everything had been looking good in Hindthorpe recently, he'd been reinstated, Openthwaite had gone, good old George had got the recognition he deserved and two of Mervyn's own projects had been successful. Did he want to change tracks now. He would still have the opportunity to work with the young people of the borough and he would have the county machine behind him, but the borough was a law unto itself, he didn't understand exactly how the politics worked. Did the borough answer to the county council? He didn't know and would have to find out. The salary Andrew mentioned was beyond his wildest dreams, but there was more to it than money. Did he want this new responsibility? He was not at all sure. He needed to talk it over with someone, but who? Not George, he wouldn't want him to go and probably wouldn't appreciate the conflict. Councillor Matthews wouldn't want him to go either, having established him in his present post. He could see what Stephanie thought, she might not be biased, as she seemed not to care one way or the other. But then, would her advice be any good? He hadn't seen Vanessa for some time, not since he had supper with her in fact, and that was months ago. Would it seem cheeky now to ask her what she thought about him leaving? He had thought there might be something going with Vanessa, she seemed to like him, and he liked her, but something had made him hesitate to move things on. What was it? He resolved to speak to her. It would serve two purposes. He would get her opinion on the new job and also be able to gauge whether or not he should try to get to know her better.

23

Mervyn phoned Vanessa as soon as he got back to his office.

'Hello, Mervyn, I thought you'd forgotten me. I haven't seen you for ages. Are you all right?'

'Yes, I am OK, just very busy. How are you? I haven't been neglecting you deliberately, in fact I've been thinking about you a lot. Could we perhaps get together?'

'What did you have in mind?'

'How about an Indian one evening?'

'Sounds nice, when?'

'Are you free tonight?'

'Yes. Do you know a good Indian? The Prince of Bengal is very good, in Everton Road?'

'I don't know it, but if you say it's good we'll go there. What shall we say – eight?'

'Half seven. Knock on my door, I'll be ready.'

Mervyn was excited at the prospect of taking Vanessa out. She had seemed quite keen and there was no awkwardness at all in making the arrangement.

Mervyn couldn't concentrate on his work for the rest of the day and by half past three in the afternoon he'd had enough and locked up his office. There was nobody about in the museum, so he just left. He had been wondering how he would deal with Stephanie if he saw her. She had been so strange at the concert, but he hadn't seen her since. Another girl had been in reception and he hadn't exchanged more than the time of day with her. He smiled. Here he was, without any female friends for ages and now there were two of them vying for his attention, or so he fantasised.

At exactly half past seven, Mervyn knocked on Vanessa's door. It opened immediately and Vanessa stepped out into the hallway, she kissed Mervyn lightly on his cheek and took his arm.

'Ready?' she said.

'Absolutely,' Mervyn replied.

They walked the two floors down to the ground floor and across to the car-park without speaking, and Mervyn held open the door of the Golf for Vanessa to get in.

In the car Mervyn looked at Vanessa and thought how nice she looked. He smiled. She smiled back.

'What?' she said.

'What do you mean?'

'You're looking at me funny again,' she laughed.

'Sorry, I can't help looking at you.'

'I don't mind, it's nice actually.' She took Mervyn's hand and squeezed it. 'Let's go,' she said.

The Indian restaurant was as good as Vanessa had said it was and they enjoyed the meal and the service immensely. Their waiter had been attentive but not intrusive, just right in fact.

While they were drinking coffee, Mervyn broached the subject of his meeting with the county youth officer and his job offer.

'What do you think? I can't make up my mind. I know it is a good offer, the money is fantastic, but I have got to like working for the council and I know my way round now. I think there is a lot I could do here. On the other hand, I am very interested in doing more for the young people, and as area youth officer I could do more. It wouldn't just be in Hindthorpe though. I would have the whole of the south of the county to deal with.'

'You wouldn't want to live in Wilson Tower, would you. Where your girlfriend lives,' Vanessa said, making a face.

Mervyn leaned across the table and took Vanessa's hand. 'My girlfriend?' he said. 'Really?'

'We're out on a date, that's what you do with your girlfriend isn't it?'

'That's it then,' Mervyn said suddenly. If you are going to be my girlfriend, I'm staying. Thank you so much!'

Vanessa laughed and smiled. They both laughed. The waiter came over.

'Is it perhaps celebration? Ve are vanting to give you drink on house. Is it?' he said.

'That would be lovely, yes, I think you could say it is a celebration,' said Mervyn.

24

Mervyn wanted to let Andrew Gooding know his decision as soon as possible. The first thing he did when he sat at his desk was phone County Hall.

'I've decided not to accept your invitation to apply for the Area Officer post, Andrew. I very much appreciate your vote of confidence and I am sure we will be able to work together, but I have decided to stay at Hindthorpe. I have established myself here and I think I can do a lot with the youth of the borough.'

'I'm very disappointed, Mervyn, but I respect your decision. I am sure we will be able to help each other. Please don't hesitate to ask me if you think I can help in any way.'

'I won't, thank you, Andrew.'

Mervyn sat back in his chair, feeling good.

A knock at his door made him sit up. 'Yes, come in.'

It was Stephanie, with a cup of coffee. 'Hello, Mervyn, how are you?' she said, as she put the cup down. 'I haven't seen you for a while.'

'No, I've been busy away from the office. How are you?'

'I'm all right. What happened to you at the concert? I looked for you afterwards and couldn't find you. Didn't you like the music?'

'It was super, but as you were preoccupied with your friends, I decided to leave early.'

'They weren't friends, they were foreign students. The chief asked me to look after them so I couldn't leave them. I'm sorry if you thought I was ignoring you. I was hoping we might go on somewhere afterwards, or perhaps to my place.'

'I'm sorry, Stephanie, I didn't know.'

'Another time?' said Stephanie.

'Sure, why not,' said Mervyn, non committally.

'See you then,' said Stephanie, leaving quietly.

That's that then, thought Mervyn, when she had gone. Another might have been, I guess.

The phone rang, making Mervyn jump. He had been daydreaming about Stephanie and Vanessa.

'Hello, Mervyn Davis, here. Can I help?'

'Hello, I think you might be able to. My name is Jeremy Felton, Reverend Jeremy Felton. I'm the minister at the Newtown Baptist Church, do you know it?'

'I know of it yes. How can I help you Mr Felton?'

'I wonder if you could come and see me?'

'Certainly, can you tell me what it's about?'

'I'd rather talk to you face to face, if that's all right.'

'Very well, when would you like to meet?'

'Tomorrow morning would suit me very well, if you are free.'

'I think I could manage that, what time?'

'Why not come for coffee, say eleven?'

'Eleven it is, I'll look forward to meeting you. Bye.'

Mervyn had not had a lot to do with Newtown, in the north of the borough, apart from his occasional visits to George's pub, the Anvil and Hammer. The north of the old town had been mostly factories in the nineteenth and twentieth centuries, but as the heavy engineering had declined and finally disappeared altogether, the factories had been demolished and acres of new housing had been put up, some said too hastily. The area had quickly got a bad reputation and it was the least desirable part of the borough in which to live. The council had not seen fit to provide facilities there with the result that the public houses were the main source of entertainment.

The Baptist Church was well known for its charismatic and evangelistic approach. Congregations on Sundays ran into many hundreds. Mervyn was intrigued by the Reverend Felton's invitation.

'Good morning, Mr Davis,' said the cleric, 'I'm delighted to see you. Come on in.'

'Good morning, I'm pleased to se you, too. Please call me Mervyn.'

'I will, and please call me Jeremy,' he smiled.

'I've asked my wife to bring us coffee, but before we have that, I would like to show you the church.'

'Oh, right you are,' said Mervyn.

Jeremy led the way into the church, which was unlike any church Mervyn had seen before. It was circular in shape, with a large stage on one side. A raised section to the side of the stage contained a baptismal pool and behind the stage was a very large illuminated cross. Large windows all around the auditorium, for that was what it essentially was, were hung with heavy velvet curtains. The whole thing had the look of a very modern theatre.

'It's amazing!' said Mervyn. 'What a wonderful building.'

'I think so, too. I'm so glad you like it. Now shall we go into my office?'

They sat in Jeremy's office and Jeremy's wife brought in the promised coffee.

'The church was built shortly after the estate was built,' began Jeremy, as he poured the coffee. 'The area, as you probably know, was completely redeveloped and intended to provide housing for the increasing numbers of immigrants coming into the borough. That didn't work out. There was a lot of trouble and eventually, by mutual consent, most of the immigrants moved to the other end of town, where most of them live today. The majority of the people who live here now are long term natives. Descendants of the people who worked in the factories. There is not a lot of work here and many of the people are unemployed. The church has done a lot to help people in difficult circumstances and as a result, or partly as a result, perhaps I should say, we have a very large congregation. What I am getting at is this. We would like to be able to provide the sort of facilities that the council provides in other parts of the town.

'Why have the council not built a community centre here?' asked Mervyn.

'You tell me. The fact is that they haven't. What I am proposing is that we build a community centre, open to all. I must emphasise that I don't want to attach any conditions to its use, but I want to build it here, on our land. We own the land already so that would reduce the cost. What I want to ask you is will the council assist us with the cost of building?'

'My initial reaction to your proposal is very positive, I must say. In the absence of any council input up to now, it would seem very reasonable to expect some financial assistance.'

'What do you think our chances are, realistically?'

'I'm afraid I cannot say. All I can do is take your suggestion to the council and see where it goes from there. I would need a very full and detailed proposal from you, with plans of the proposed building. Have you had plans drawn up?'

'Only some outline drawings and artist's impressions so far. Full drawings are very expensive as I'm sure you know, and before we spend any money we need to know if the council is going to come in with us or if we are going to have to go it alone. We do intend to build this centre, come what may.'

'If you could let me have copies of what drawings you do have I will do my best to get the idea in front of the relevant people.'

'Thank you, that is all I could expect at this stage. So you think it is a good idea?'

'I do. I do indeed. A very good idea.'

Mervyn was not sure who he should talk to about the church community centre. He would try to find out why the council had not already provided a community centre and if they had any plans to build one. He thought if there were any Christian councillors, they would be the ones to talk to first, but how to find out who they might be.'

25

Mervyn was quite excited with the proposals for a new community centre in Newtown, and went back to the museum, hoping to put the idea to the chief.

Stephanie was in reception, looking radiant. Mervyn hadn't seen her for a while, but hadn't asked where she was in case his enquiry had been misconstrued. Now, it seemed clear where she had been as she was sporting a wonderful tan. Her fair skin had gone a glorious golden colour and her already fair hair had been bleached by the sun. She looking stunning and Mervyn's heart missed a beat when he saw her.

'Hello, Mervyn,' she called, as he walked through the foyer. 'How are you?'

'I'm well, thank you, Stephanie, and I don't need to ask how you are. You are the picture of health. You look wonderful.'

'Thank you, kind sir. I've been to the Caribbean. It was fantastic.'

'I've always wanted to go to the West Indies myself but could never afford it. I'm glad you had a good time.'

'Shall I bring you a cup of coffee? I could show you my photographs.'

'That would be nice, thanks. I'm hoping to see the chief. Is he in?'

'Not until this afternoon. We've got all the morning,' she said, suggestively.

Mervyn went though to his office and a few minutes later Stephanie came in with a tray of coffee and biscuits and a stack of colour photographs. She poured the coffee and added milk and sugar for Mervyn and sat next to him so she could show him her photographs.

Most of them seemed to be of Stephanie herself, dressed appropriately for the sun in a very brief bikini. She was a lovely looking young woman and Mervyn found himself wondering what might have been if only he had stayed around on the night of the concert. He sensed that Stephanie was deliberately teasing him with the pictures of her near naked body.

'They're lovely, Stephanie, it looks fantastic. I'm so pleased to had a good holiday.'

'What do you want to see the chief about, Mervyn? Have you got another project in mind?' Stephanie asked.

'Well, yes I have as a matter of fact. It might come to nothing but I'll be interested to see what the chief makes of it.'

'Can you tell me about it, or is it a secret?' asked Stephanie, still sitting uncomfortably close, and looking into Mervyn's eyes.

'No, it isn't a secret exactly, but I would rather you didn't tell anyone about it until I have discussed it with the chief. You know there isn't a community Centre in Newtown? Well the minister of the Baptist church up there wants to build a centre in the church grounds. He wants it to be open to everyone and he would like some help from the council to build it. I think it sounds good, and they certainly need something on that estate.'

'You know why there isn't anything up there do you?' asked Stephanie, looking suddenly serious.

'No, why is that?'

'Well, when the factories were all closed down and demolished, and the new houses built, the council at the time promised to set up new businesses to employ the people who had been factory workers. The houses were built and a lot of immigrants moved in . . .'

'Yes, I had heard that, but they moved out again.'

'That's right, but the new businesses never materialised and the people were up in arms. There was a lot of trouble but the council didn't seem to want to know. Ever since then Newtown has been firmly Liberal.'

'What, in protest, you mean?'

'That's what it was to start with, they refused to support the Labour council because they had let them down. They couldn't vote Tory obviously – so they elected a Liberal councillor. And they have done ever since. The council has been predominantly Labour for years of course and they won't do anything for Newtown. That's why it's such a dump.'

'That is interesting. How come you know so much about it?'

'I did it all at college. I did my thesis on Politics and Social Unrest of the Twentieth Century.'

'Clever as well,' mumbled Mervyn, looking afresh at the delectable Stephanie.

'What was that, Mervyn?' she said.

'Oh, nothing. You're a clever girl, Stephanie. Thanks for the lecture. It explains a lot. So, you don't think this plan has a lot of mileage then?'

'I wouldn't have thought so, but it's worth a go. Best of luck.' She smiled and picked up the empty cups and saucers and left the office. Leaving Mervyn with a lot to think about.

Mervyn was pleased he had the benefit of knowledge of the history of Newtown when he presented the idea of the community centre to the chief later that day.

'I fear your idea is already dead in the water, Mervyn,' said the chief, with a wry smile. 'All manner of projects have been mooted for Newtown over the years, and the council just throws them out. They say if Newtown would like to vote Labour, things might change. But you know how awkward people can be. They'd rather do without than go back on their principles. I suggest you have a quiet word with your friend Matthews, see what he says. But really, I don't think you stand a chance. Well done for trying though.'

As both Stephanie and the chief had predicted, the idea of a church led community centre did not meet with approval. The immediate reaction was, again as predicted, if Newtown residents voted Liberal, what could they expect, this is a Labour administration. The solution is in their hands. Then, just to make sure the coffin was securely nailed down, they raised the religious objection. As the Baptist church was Christian it would be inaccessible to the many adherents of other religions in the borough, and it might offend some of them. Mervyn had tried to say that there was absolutely no intention on the part of the church to make use the centre in any way conditional on anyone's faith or, for that matter, lack of it. But his protestations fell on deaf ears. He was very disappointed and hated having to go to see the very nice Reverend Jeremy Felton to tell him that the council would not consider his proposal.

'I have to say, I am not really surprised, Mervyn. There are none so deaf as those who do not wish to listen. I will not give up though. If necessary we'll go ahead on our own. We'll need to raise more money if we do it ourselves but I am sure that, with God on our side, we will succeed.' The cleric smiled and shook Mervyn's hand warmly. 'You would be most welcome to join us on a Sunday morning, Mervyn. Think about it.' He smiled again. Mervyn smiled and they left good friends.

26

Mervyn took stock of his achievements while driving back to the museum. He'd had a few mishaps and a few run-ins with awkward people, but on the whole he had done well. He had established an embryonic youth service in the borough – he'd even been offered a job in the youth service. He'd got a go-kart track up and running and a new youth centre was almost ready to open, with the prospect of more in the near future. He'd made friends with a lot of people and he'd even got himself a girlfriend. He very nearly had two girlfriends. He smiled to himself at that.

As he drove into the car-park at the museum, he was still smiling. The groundsman gave him a cheery wave as he passed, perhaps thinking the smile was directed at him.

He entered the museum and waved and smiled at Stephanie in reception. He waved and smiled at the curator, who was struggling with a new display in the foyer.

'There was a phone message for you, Mervyn. A serious water leak in Wilson Tower, will you see to it?' said Stephanie, handing him a note.

'I'll see to it,' he said, confidently. I'm the man from the council, he thought.

Lightning Source UK Ltd.
Milton Keynes UK
UKOW01f0750310117
293247UK00001B/8/P

9 781786 976161